JN260209

The Truth
Never Hitherto Disclosed

*On the Hereafter,
and the Past, Present,
and Future of the Earth*

Nichijo

たま出版

Prologue

"Where do we come from? what are we? where are we going?"

You may have heard this famous quote, which serves as the title of a piece by the painter Paul Gauguin. I'm sure that all of my readers have at one time or another asked these same questions themselves, wondering whence humankind has come, why we are here, and what will happen to us when we die.

Even today, in an age when scientific advancement greatly enriches our daily lives, scientists, philosophers, and even religious leaders have been unable to produce satisfactory answers. Even those who claim to have found the answers can provide only vague and difficult ones. Because we do not have clear answers to these questions, many in our times have lost sight of the purpose of life. So they live in fear of death and disease, wracked with worry, suffering, and anxieties about the future.

The answers to these questions are incredibly profound. While there are not enough pages in this book to cover everything, I would like to share at least a part of it with my readers, in a way that is easy to understand. Even while only one part is covered, I believe that readers will be somewhat shocked to find that, after reading this book, things that they never understood before become clear to them. You may be surprised at how clearly and concretely you can understand those things.

I would like to explain briefly how I came to write this book. The truth is that the content of this book is based on what was taught to me by God, the Creator, maker of the universe and Earth, as well as humanity, animals, plants, and all matter and life.

There may be many Japanese who tend to steer clear of the idea of God or other deities. I used to be one of those people. Just a few years ago, I was running a small business. Before that, I was a very run-of-the-mill office worker. Especially when I was a child, I led a life that was completely unconnected to God, thinking, "How am I supposed to know if God exists or not?" and that, if God did exist, it would have to be only in my mind.

But when I was 20, I was made to know the existence of God and other deities. After that, I was taught that there are grand workings of the universe, including the worlds after death, and that I have a critical destiny (a mission) that I have been assigned by God. That mission is to bring the truths, which God has revealed to me, to all of the people living now who have forgotten the existence of deities.

My life, before I understood my mission, was full of ups and downs. There was nothing like smooth sailing. I've had my share of hardships and trials. I was even duped into incurring debts for others. But when I learned of the important destiny that I was given by God, I was able to understand the life that I had led up to then, and I learned that there is nothing in this world for nothing. In order to pass on God's teachings to people in all circumstances and from all walks of life, I had to become someone who could sympathize with people and understand their pain. If I were someone who never knew hardships and trials, I would not be able to truly understand the feelings of those in pain. Were I to attempt to spread the teachings of God to people without ever knowing hardships and trials, the message would ring hollow no matter how brilliant the teachings of God are.

When God gave me my important destiny, my life was changed completely. I left my business to my colleagues, and I moved from Chiba Prefecture to Gifu, Japan, with my family. Then I began my preparations for carrying out my destiny.

Some years ago, I met a special spiritual counselor. That counselor is able to speak freely with deities through channeling. I have met many counselors, but her channeling is more accurate than any other I've met. And when she asks deities a question, a clear and definite answer comes right then and there.

There are many elements in the teachings I have received from God, and they include the true history from the appearance of humankind to the present day, the true form of the universe, the worlds after death, and the direction that Earth and humankind are heading in. My wish is to bring these truths to as many people as possible, in a way that they can understand, and I want them to take these truths as signs of how to live going forward.

I am currently engaged in holding lectures all over Japan, where I pass on God's teachings. But as there are things that can't be fully explained in the time-frame of a lecture, I decided to set down in more detail what we talk about in the lectures. It isn't difficult to understand the content of this book. So I would like everyone, children and adults alike, to read it.

The existence of deities and the truths have been revealed to me, and have been substantiated for me by strange and mysterious happenings and miracles, which I have experienced time and again. I won't go into all the details of each and every one of these experiences, but I have seen multitudes of strange happenings and miracles that most people could never imagine.

Sometimes the teachings of God seem to go against the normal common sense of the world. And depending on circumstances, there may seem to be from a human perspective, some contradictions. For that reason, I'm sure that many of you reading this book right now will have doubts about whether it's all true or not. There have been times when even I myself wondered at first whether the things that God taught me were true.

But later, you will surely come to understand that everything is in accordance with God's teachings. I can say this with confidence based on my own various experiences up to now. Since these teachings, in one sense, contain information that predicts things to come in this age, there are also things that seem to go against common knowledge, but these things in time will become common knowledge. That is why I would like to ask the readers of this book to approach it with a clean, pure heart without any preconceptions.

I'm sure that, if you come to understand that deities exist and that there are grand workings of the universe, your life from here on out will be completely different. I am praying with all my heart that this book will be the opening chapter of a brilliant life for you.

Table of Contents

Prologue ... 1

Chapter 1 The Real History:
From the Dawn of Humanity to Modern Civilization

1-1 The truth about the birthplace of humanity ... 10
1-2 From the birth of humanity to great civilizations ... 12
1-3 From the Mu civilization to the current civilization ... 13
1-4 Ruins of Mu all over the world ... 17
1-5 What we can learn from Mu ... 22

Chapter 2 The True Workings of the Universe and Humanity

2-1 Why speak of the worlds after death? ... 28
2-2 The true form of the universe we live in ... 29
2-3 The true structure of the human body as revealed to me by God ... 33
2-4 Human reincarnation ... 37

Chapter 3 The Workings of Human Reincarnation

3-1 The Spirit Realm ... 42
3-2 A general overview of reincarnation and transmigration ... 47
3-3 How we are born into the Present Realm ... 54
3-4 The significance of birth in this world ... 59
   Column: Your destined soul mate ... 64
3-5 Leaving the Present Realm ... 65
3-6 The true significance of the 49-day period and divine judgment ... 75
3-7 Atonement in the Astral Realm, and then to the Spirit Realm ... 81
3-8 The issues of organ donation and transplants ... 92
3-9 On suicide: the importance of living every moment ... 97

Chapter 4 The Future of Earth and Humanity

- 4-1   The state of Earth ·· 106
- 4-2   Towards the evolution of Earth and humankind ························ 115
- 4-3   Our environment: climate change and natural disasters ··············· 120
        Column: Insects and animals predicting the future?! ··············· 124
- 4-4   Economic and social conditions ·· 125
        Column: Tokyo Skytree ·· 130
- 4-5   The movement of infectious diseases ···································· 131
- 4-6   How to survive: the importance of living with a righteous heart ····· 146

In Closing ·· 151

Chapter 1

The Real History: From the Dawn of Humanity to Modern Civilization

1-1 The truth about the birthplace of humanity

"When, where, and how did humanity appear on the face of this Earth?"

We can imagine a number of origins, from evolving from monkeys to increasing from Adam and Eve, who were made by God.

According to the latest scientific theories based on various fossils records, the birth of humanity is placed on the African continent, some 7 million years ago. The theory goes that, while humankind has some common ancestors with anthropoid apes like chimpanzees, gorillas, and orangutans, about 7 million years ago on the African continent, there was a sudden genetic change only in humankind, through which we obtained the characteristics of erect bipedalism (walking upright on two legs) and a shortening of the canines (the fangs). This type of evolutionary theory is accepted by many in our age as a scientific explanation.

Judging from purely physical characteristics, it is indeed true that the closest animal to humans is the chimpanzee. That is why we also tend to think that humans and chimpanzees had common ancestors, and were separated by the process of evolu-

Chapter 1 The Real History

tion.

Humans and animals are composed of visible physical bodies and invisible souls (spirits), but the human soul is fundamentally different from the animal one. That is why humans are humans and chimpanzees are chimpanzees, and why millions of years from now chimpanzees will not become smarter to build civilizations like those of humankind. The theory of evolution is not entirely correct about the origin of humanity.

What, then, is the answer to the question we posed at the beginning of this section?

I was informed of the answer by God. This is what he taught me:

Humanity began in its current physical form about 5 million years ago, in what is now the city of Kofu in Yamanashi Prefecture, Japan.

"Current physical form" means with bodies exactly the same as those we have now. That is to say, not those who had bodies covered with fur like a chimpanzee or those still somewhat hunched up, having just evolved from quadrupeds. Further, the first of humankind, rather than being born on

Earth as someone's child, descended from a place called the Spirit Realm as fully developed adults.[1]

[1] The Spirit Realm will be dealt with in detail in the next chapter.

1-2 From the birth of humanity to great civilizations

At the time when humankind first appeared, the layout of Earth was completely different. Surprisingly, Japan was a part of the continent of Mu, that continent of legend which, in spite of the glory of a great civilization comparable to our own, sank into the Pacific Ocean. That is to say, Japan is what is left of the sunken continent of Mu. The continent of Atlantis also

● **The continents as they were when humankind first appeared**

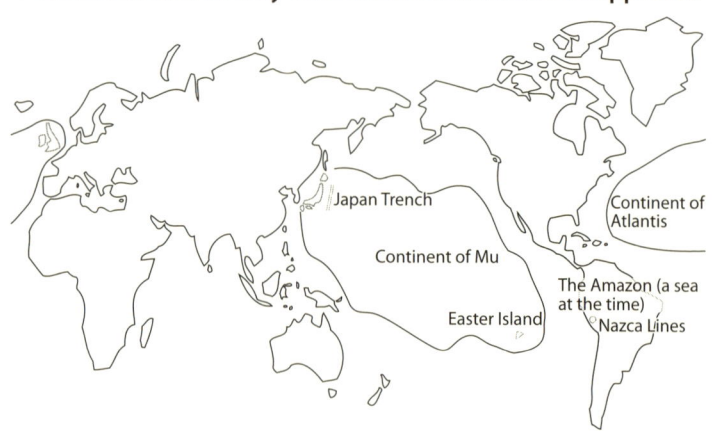

Chapter 1 The Real History

existed at that time, in the Atlantic Ocean.

The first humans in the world, who descended to the present-day location of Kofu in Yamanashi roughly 5 million years ago, then a part of the continent of Mu, were a race with yellow skin. In about 100,000 years after the appearance of this yellow race, God created races of other colors,

● **The five-colored fukinagashi**

in the following order: red, blue, white, and black. The five-colored fukinagashi (windsocks) or nobori (banners) often seen used at shrines actually represent these five different races (together signifying all humanity). Moreover, as humankind was still immature when it first appeared, deities provided them with direct guidance. Then, after an immensely long period of time, humankind built its great civilization, that is, the great civilization of the Mu Empire.

1-3 From the Mu civilization to the current civilization

The civilization of the Mu Empire reached its zenith of glory tens of thousands of years ago. It achieved scientific progress comparable to our own. Surprisingly, that civilization used atomic energy, built rockets, and even traveled into space. It also created many enormous stone statues of kings and deities.

Out of the entire continent of Mu, the center of its flourishing civilization was located in what is now Kofu, Yamanashi. From there, humankind moved to the southern parts of the continent of Mu, and then to all other parts of the world. The yellow race settled in the southeast of Asia, including China and Taiwan, with Japan at the center. The red race went to settle in the Middle East, the blue race in Russia and northwestern Europe, the white race in Europe, and the black race in Africa. This being the case, Japan (the Mu Empire) was the center for the birth of humanity, and the rise of civilization. In this sense, Japan is the oldest divinely sovereign nation in the world.

However, the glory of the Mu civilization did not last forever. Roughly 12,000 years ago, the continent of Mu disappeared without a trace into the Pacific Ocean, and the Mu civilization became extinct.[2] The direct cause of the sinking of Mu was the massive explosion of the gas chambers beneath the continent. Nearly all of the people of the Mu Empire were killed as a result of this huge explosion. The archipelago of Japan that we know today is one part that barely escaped sink-

Chapter 1 The Real History

ing. The Japan Trench that still remains to this day is an enormous crack that formed when Mu sank. Because of this, there are many vestiges of the Mu era that can still be seen in Japan. For example, about 48 percent of the contemporary Japanese vocabulary actually comes from the language of Mu. The traditional dress of the Japanese people, the kimono, was also originally the style of clothing worn during the Mu era. The Mu Empire also took the lotus flower as its national flower, because it was the first flower that bloomed on the face of this Earth. There were many pyramids and artifacts of the Mu Empire in Japan, but over the long span of time that has passed, these have been lost due to human activity.

●**Lotus flowers**

Other islands now found in the Pacific Ocean, including the Hawaiian Islands, the Mariana Islands, and Easter Island, were all peaks of the mountains that towered over the continent of Mu, and these also barely escaped sinking. This is why these islands all have gigantic ruins and carvings of stone, and also have many cultural features in common. There is also a common legend of a Great Flood. On the contrary, however, the Amazon region of South America used to be a sea until the continent of Mu sank, but it was propelled to rise above the surface and became wetlands and marshes.

After the devastating sinking of the continent of Mu, those left alive in Japan and on other islands in the Pacific were unable to maintain the advanced level of science and technology. So everything went back to a completely primitive lifestyle. After that, all of the people who had moved on to other parts of the world from the continent of Mu were also sent back to square one to rebuild civilization. From there, they progressed towards our current civilization. That is to say, our current civilization is the second highly scientifically advanced civilization to exist on Earth.

This is the scientific aspect of how the Mu civilization was destroyed. In actuality though, there was a deeper cause for its extinction. The people of that era forgot the existence of deities, who had made and guided them; they chased after money and material possessions, seeking only extravagance; becoming overly confident, they began to lead self-centered lives, and destroyed nature; the hearts and souls of humanity became wicked. God and other deities, much aggrieved by the situation, completely destroyed the Mu civilization by causing that continent to sink into the ocean. As a result, nearly all of the

Chapter 1 The Real History

people alive in that era perished, excluding the very few pure-hearted who had been chosen by deities.

This is the true history as revealed to me by God. Believe it or not, it's absolutely true.

---

[2] The continent of Atlantis, located in the Atlantic Ocean, sank into the sea around 5,000 years after Mu sank.

1-4 Ruins of Mu all over the world

(1) The truth about the Moai statues

I'm sure you've heard of the Moai statues of Easter Island.

The Moai statues are monolithic statues of human faces made of stone. About 1,000 of them can be found on this island, ranging from the shortest at 3 meters (about 10 feet) to the tallest at 22 meters (about 70 feet) in height. There are many mysteries surrounding these Moai statues, but God taught me the reason for their construction.

About 10 years before the sinking of Mu, God ordered the Emperor of Mu, Rongo, to construct these monolithic statues of human faces to inform future generations of the presence of the great civilization in the Pacific. Rongo then commissioned

● The Moai statues of Easter Island

an artist named Moai to make the stone faces, thus the statues still bear the artist's name today.

There are many archaeological theories of how these Moai were made, but the most commonly accepted among them is that they were carved from rock (tuffaceous rock) in the mountains on the island, then placed horizontally on wooden sleds, and pulled by a great number of people using ropes. When the destination was reached, they were set upright using levers. The truth, however, is different.

As Mu had a technologically and scientifically advanced culture, there were of course trucks and cranes, as in modern times. The Moai statues were created using these. Moreover, iron cutting tools also existed as they do today, but as iron tools would leave hard, severe edges, Moai decided to use stone tools instead of iron tools.

Most of the Moai statues are lined up facing the mountains. This represents the worship of deities who are believed to inhabit those mountains. Only seven of them face the ocean. These seven were made to face the cities of Mu, the father of all nations, soon to sink. Now that the cities of Mu are at the bottom of the ocean, these Moai statues gaze out at the water.

(2) The truth about the Nazca Lines

The Nazca Lines are a number of figures and drawings of plants and animals on the ground of a high, dry plateau between the Nazca and Ingenio rivers in Peru. These geoglyphs have been called the oldest mysteries in human history, and range from the smallest at around 10 meters (about 30 feet) across to the largest, which stretches over 50 kilometers (about 30 miles).

The geoglyphs were discovered in the late 1930s. Airplanes had already been invented by the time these figures were discovered, which enabled to confirm what the lines looked like from above.

- The Nazca Lines (Condor)

- Satellite photo of the largest geoglyph
  (A white line is used here to show the lines more clearly.)

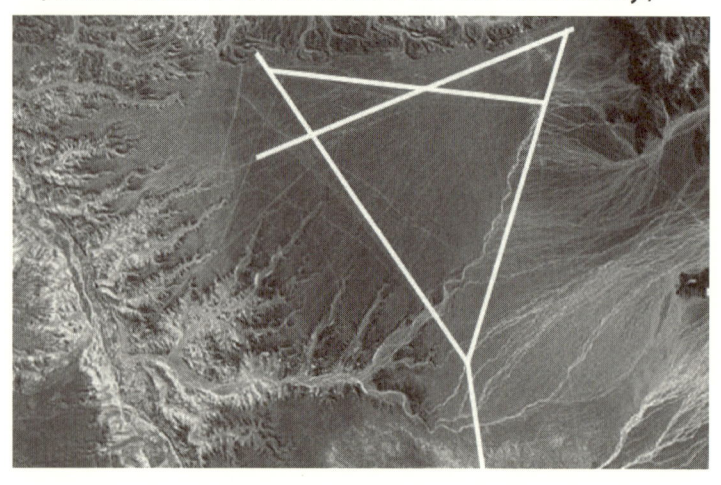

Chapter 1 The Real History

- **Yonaguni Monument (main terrace)
 From the Wonder Okinawa Website (Okinawa Prefecture)
 http://www.wonder-okinawa.jp/024/japanese/index.html**

The largest of these geoglyphs, in the shape of an arrow stretching over 50 kilometers (about 30 miles), was discovered recently by NASA's Landsat imaging satellite. This figure is made on a scale that can be discerned way above the height of the stratosphere at an altitude of 900 kilometers (about 560 miles). The technologies to measure and engineer these figures are thought to be unmistakably equivalent or superior to today's cutting edge technologies.

For what purpose were these geoglyphs created in Nazca?

God taught me that these geoglyphs are in fact another work of the Mu era. These were also drawn in order to make the presence of this great civilization be known to future generations. Surprisingly, these geoglyphs were actually drawn from the air using UFOs.

(3) Underwater ruins in areas of Okinawa

At the bottom of the ocean, just south of Yonaguni Island in Okinawa Prefecture, Japan, rest a variety of ruins. These ruins, with their stone structures of terraces and platforms, clearly created by human hands, speak to the fact that the once glorious Mu Empire sank deep to the bottom of the ocean, and that Japan was once a part of the continent of Mu.

1-5 What we can learn from Mu

Some of my readers may have already noticed that the people who lived in the end times of the Mu civilization were strikingly similar to the people of today.

People in our time push for mass production and mass consumption based on their ideology of placing economic value above all else, seeking nothing but money, material objects, and abundance. Almost as if to show that they can do anything they want as long as there is profit to be made, people have cut

Chapter 1 The Real History

down countless forests, polluted rivers and oceans by dumping waste from factories in them, and pumped large volumes of carbon dioxide into the air by burning fossil fuels, selfishly destroying Earth's environment. Global warming is the result. In recent years, natural disasters thought to be brought about by global warming have been occurring one after another. There have been more heat waves and cold waves, gigantic typhoons, sudden torrential downpours, massive flooding, droughts, and tornadoes than we can count. The areas where various infectious diseases occur are expanding due to large-scale changes in climate caused by global warming.

When we trace these phenomena back to their source, we find that it is indeed because people's hearts have gone astray. Selfish people have grown in number, and Earth's environment is beyond repair. That selfishness is now coming back to haunt us. That is to say, all of these phenomena occurring now have been caused by the condition of our hearts and minds.

As I will discuss in more detail in Chapter 4, in a sense, this means that God and other deities are causing more natural disasters (such as huge earthquakes and eruptions) and infectious diseases in order to warn humanity that their hearts and minds have strayed too far. I'm sure there are many of you who can recall the new strain of influenza (H1N1) that first reared its head in Mexico in the spring of 2009, as well as the foot-and-mouth disease that caused severe damage to livestock in Miyazaki Prefecture, Japan, from spring to summer of 2010. We have to be aware that conditions are presently very similar to those that caused the extinction of the Mu civilization, and that if we keep going this way our current civilization will also, unquestionably, become extinct, and many will perish.

So why have people's hearts strayed?

This is because the people of today have forgotten God who made them, and now mistakenly believe only in the visible world.

If this visible world is all there is, then there is no world after death, and when we die it is the end. When people believe that, after we die, we completely cease to be, and that we only live once, it's natural that they will want to live the most interesting, fun and extravagant lives they can. That's why a great number of people think that they can disregard others completely, as long as it's good for them and it's good for now; they seek only money, objects, and abundance.

But death is not the end for us. In God's grand scheme, even after we die, we are conscious and have senses the same as

Chapter 1 The Real History

we have when alive.

In the following chapters, I would like to discuss in detail the structure of the universe, which includes the realms beyond death.

Chapter 2

The True Workings of the Universe and Humanity

2-1 Why speak of the worlds after death?

As we discussed in the last chapter, the environment of Earth has reached the breaking point. It would be no exaggeration to say that Earth is now literally crying out in pain. If we continue to carry on, as we have, and do not repent, humanity will continue to experience large-scale natural disasters and a variety of infectious diseases, and many lives will be lost cataclysmically. Then, the curtain will close on global civilization.

I believe, however, that if enough people learn of the true structure and workings of this universe, including the realms beyond death, and change their hearts, the world will take a turn for the better. Even if it's impossible now to stop the extinction of civilization, God will surely delay the final days of our civilization if we can transform our hearts. The later the last day comes, the more people can transcend the extinction of this culture and survive.

To spread this news to as many people as possible by the time the last day comes, and to save as many people as possible—this is exactly my motivation for holding lectures all over Japan to speak on the realms beyond death, and also for writing this book.

Chapter 2 The True Workings of the Universe and Humanity

I am often asked by participants in my lectures why I know so much about the realms beyond death. In Chapters 2 and 3 of this book, I will explain these realms beyond death in more detail than I do in my lectures. So I'm sure there will be many readers who have the same sort of doubts when they finish reading.

Since there has been no religion up to now that describes the realms beyond death in this amount of detail, it's no surprise that people should wonder where it came from. But what I share with you all in this book and in my lectures is not just something that I dreamed up myself, but something taught to me by God who is the Creator of the universe, our Earth, and all life. That's why I am able to describe the structure and workings of the realms in such detail. In the remainder of this chapter, I will provide my readers with an overview of the true form of the universe, the true composition of the human body, and human reincarnation.

2-2 The true form of the universe we live in

The universe in which we live is not made up of only visible space. In actuality, other spaces invisible to the eye also exist as part of the universe. The entire universe consists of one-dimensional to seven-dimensional spaces.

● **The structure of the universe**

Seven-dimensional space	Realm of Deity (where deities abide)
Six-dimensional space	
Five-dimensional space	
Four-dimensional space	Spirit Realm (the home and origin of the human soul; so-called Heaven)
	Astral Realm (where sins are atoned for after death; so-called Hell)
Three-dimensional space	Present Realm (the material world—Earth, humanity, plants, and animals)
Two-dimensional space	Uninhabited by living things (unrelated worlds)
One-dimensional space	

In more detail, there exist, in this universe, places called the Present Realm, the Astral Realm, the Spirit Realm, and the Realm of Deity. These will each be explained in order below.

First of all, the Present Realm is "this world," also known as the material world. The Present Realm is described as three-dimensional space. This is the place in which we humans, along with plants and animals, are born, live out our lives, and eventually die.

The Astral Realm and the Spirit Realm make up the so-called the other side. These are described as four-dimensional space, and are invisible to people living in the Present Realm. The Astral Realm, so-called Hell, is where people atone for the sins of their lives.[3] If we wished to compare it to something in the Present Realm, we could think of it as a prison. Next, the Spirit Realm, so-called Heaven, is a place where we live before we are born into the Present Realm. This is also the place where those who lived free from sin go directly when they die. Since our souls are originally created in the Spirit Realm, it could be properly called the "home and origin of the human soul."

Unfortunately, many people commit sins in their lives, which results in being sent to the Astral Realm (Hell) after they die. However, if they sincerely repent their sins, and abandon their attachments to the Present Realm (this world), God and other deities will forgive them, and they may return to the Spirit Realm (Heaven).

Many of you might have heard of heaven and hell, and wondered if places like those could really exist. The truth is that heaven and hell are not just devices or parables; they actually exist. There may be many of you who think that, when we die, it's all over, and that there's nothing more. Many of those who think this way are afraid of death.

But it's not all over when we die. On the contrary, compared to the amount of time we spend in this world, the time we spend in the other worlds is much longer. Furthermore, our actions in the Present Realm determine where we go in the afterlife. The sins that we commit in this world will be judged fairly by deities, and we are made to reflect upon them in the Astral Realm.

Even though we use the word "sin," this isn't limited to such heinous crimes as thievery and murder. Even actions that many people in this world may find insignificant, like littering with cigarette butts or jaywalking, will not be overlooked by deities. They give us suitable punishments in the afterlife, wondering why we can't keep ourselves from breaking even the simplest rules, condemning those who would sin so lightly.

The final place that makes up the universe, the Realm of Deity, is described as a five-, six-, or seven-dimensional space, which is of course invisible to the human eye. As its name suggests, the Realm of Deity is the place where God and other deities God and gods live.

These various places, however, do not exist completely independently of each other. These realms exist in the same space, and parts of them overlap and can influence one another. This is why various types of supernatural events (ghost sightings, rapping sounds, etc.) occur in the material world. There are those who dismiss them out of hand as "paranormal phenomena" but the fact is that what happens in either the

Astral Realm, the Spirit Realm, or the Realm of Deity, may come through to this world.

[3] "To atone for sins" means to acknowledge one's sins, and to reflect upon them sincerely.

2-3 The true structure of the human body as revealed to me by God

Physical body, astral body, and spirit body

Just as, in the universe, the visible world and the invisible realms exist layered upon one another, so too is the human body constructed of a visible physical body and invisible astral and spirit bodies, making a total of three layers.

To put it simply, the physical body is for use in the Present Realm, the astral body is for use in the Astral Realm, and the spirit body is for use in the Spirit Realm.

To use a simple analogy, the spirit body is in the center of your body. The astral body is like a costume you wear over your spirit body, and the physical body is like a costume you wear on top of that. That is probably the easiest way to picture the human body. So, as soon as we die, we take off costume, the physical body at first, and spend time using our astral body. Then later, after finishing atonement in the Astral Realm, and

● The human body

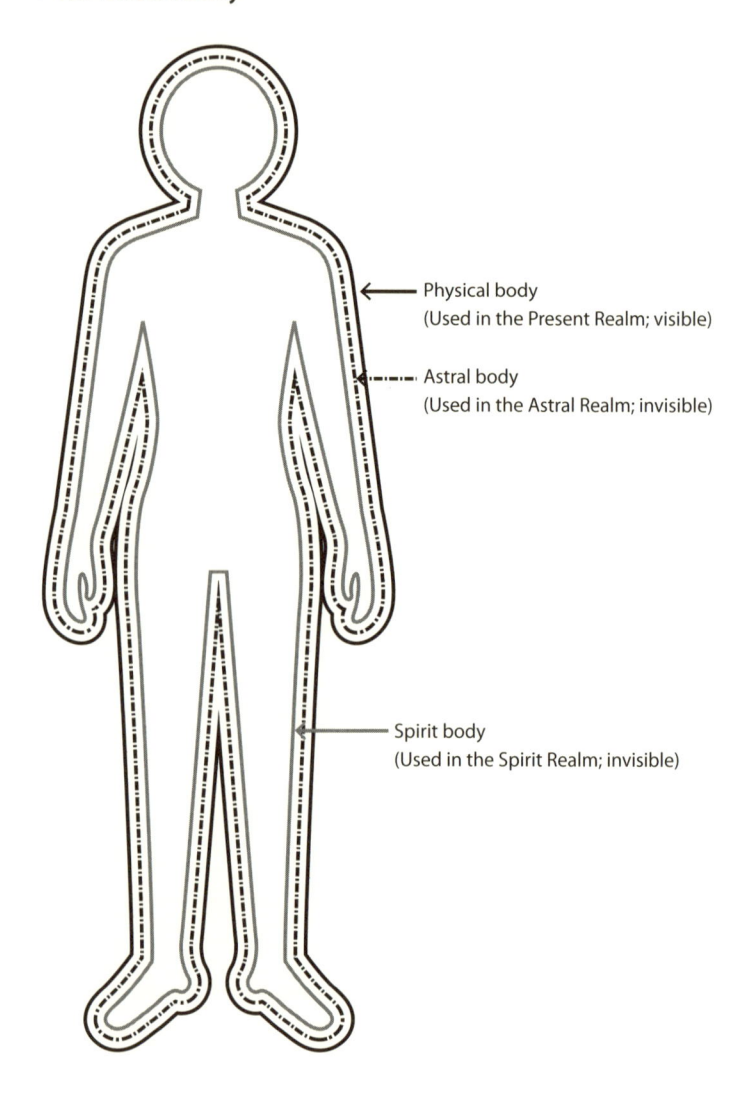

← Physical body
(Used in the Present Realm; visible)

←·—·— Astral body
(Used in the Astral Realm; invisible)

← Spirit body
(Used in the Spirit Realm; invisible)

just before making our return to the Spirit Realm, we also shed the costume of our astral body, and go back to live using our spirit body as the original form in the Spirit Realm.

On human souls

We as humans are able to remember things, and to think and create. These abilities are inherent in our souls (our original spirits). The human soul sits in the pineal gland of the spirit body, and drives the functions of the entire body (physical, astral, and spirit). The pineal gland is situated in a place about 10 centimeters (about 4 inches) to the inside of the forehead in adults, and it's a pinecone-shaped structure about 1 centimeter (about half an inch) in diameter. This shape is in fact how this structure has its name. Medically, it is considered to be a gland that secretes hormones.

To use a vehicle as an analogy, we could think of the soul as a driver, and the pineal gland as the driver's seat. And the physical body is the vehicle used in the Present Realm, the astral body is the vehicle used in the Astral Realm, and the spirit body is the vehicle used in the Spirit Realm.

On the appearance of the physical, astral, and spirit bodies

The appearance (facial features, race, etc.) of the physical and astral bodies are exactly the same. The astral body ages as

● **The location of the pineal gland**

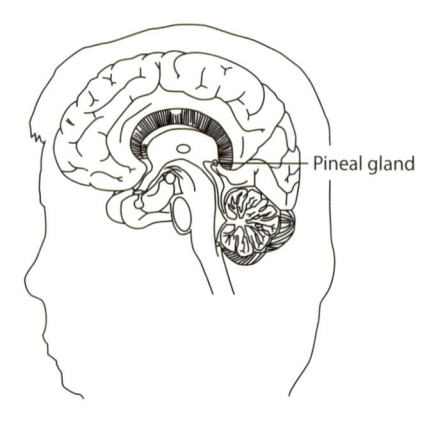

Pineal gland

the physical body does. Further, any wounds or illness inflicted on the physical body will also be reflected just the same on the astral body. Those who end their lives in the severe pain that comes with terminal cancer, for example, will continue on in pain, as their astral bodies also have terminal cancer. This is why it's not correct to think that dying will release us from pain.[4] In fact, on top of it, we have to atone for our sins in the Astral Realm in this state as well. For this reason, it is very important for us to die peacefully, without pain.

The spirit body, on the other hand, is unaffected no matter what kind of illness or injury we suffer to our physical and astral bodies. Our spirit bodies retain the youth of a 20-year-old forever, and never age at all. No matter what race or ethnicity a person's physical body takes on, their spirit body is a member of the "yellow" race. As described in the previous chapter, God created five different races in the age of the Mu Empire millennia ago. God gave humanity different colored skin in the Present Realm in order that we should practice living in harmony with one another. However, as the Spirit Realm is no place for that sort of practice, the spirit bodies of all humanity are of the yellow race.

[4] By coming to realize, and reflect upon, our sins in the Astral Realm, the pain that remains after death will be softened little by little.

2-4 Human reincarnation

Humans are born again and again. After dying, atoning for sins in the Astral Realm, and then returning to the Spirit Realm, we come back to be born once again in this world. This is called *reincarnation*.

So how long does it take for a person to be reborn?

This depends on the person. It's normal to be reborn 1,000 years after the death in the material world, but it can be as little as 300 to 400 years. There are others whose life in the Spirit Realm is extended, and they may require a period of something

- **Appearance of the physical body, astral body, and spirit body**
  (Though invisible to the eye, the body is in fact composed of these three-layered bodies.)

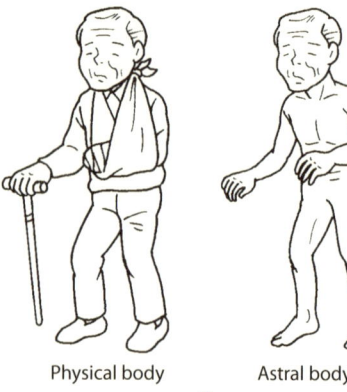

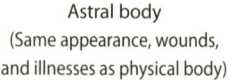

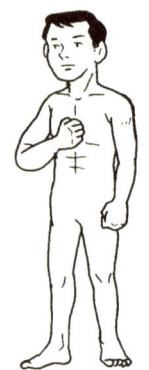

Physical body	Astral body	Spirit body
	(Same appearance, wounds, and illnesses as physical body)	(Free of damage and disease; youth of a 20-year-old)

more like 10,000 years before being reborn.

Furthermore, every time a person is reborn into this world, their physical and astral bodies have a completely different appearance from that in their previous life. For example when a person is reborn as Japanese, they have the physical and astral bodies of the yellow race, and, when they are born as an African, they have the physical and astral body of the black race. In this sense, we should think of these physical and astral bodies we get with each reincarnation, as temporary bodies. Your spirit body, on the other hand, never changes no matter how many times you repeat the process of reincarnation, and it is your true body.

Fundamentally, humans are born into this world as humans. There are rare cases, however, in which people are born as animals in this world. That means that their soul is human, but their physical bodies are that of the animal they have been born as. (The astral body in this case is also animal, but the spirit body is human.) This is called *transmigration*.

Seeing-Eye dogs are one good example of humans transmigrated as animals. Because their souls are human, Seeing-Eye dogs are able to better understand human language. Other pets (dogs, cats, and so on) that keep turning up at your house no matter how many times you try to get rid of them are usually transmigrations of ancestors.

In this way, we all move back and forth between three-dimensional Present Realm and four-dimensional Astral and Spirit Realms, repeating this cycle of reincarnation and transmigration (transmigration depends on the person; so there are individuals who do not experience it).[5] This cycle is known to Buddhists as *samsara*, or simply as cyclical reincarnation.

But why do we have to repeat this cycle of birth, death, and rebirth?

It is so that, through being reborn over and over again in the Present Realm, we gain practice by leading a variety of lives, and thus cultivate our souls.

As described previously, the human soul is created initially in the Spirit Realm. Thereafter, it continues to be cultivated through repeated reincarnations. You, with this book in your hand right now, are also in fact in the middle of this process.

In the next chapter, I would like to address human reincarnation in more detail.

---

[5] Transmigration is fundamentally something that we are made to experience in order to atone for sins in a previous life.

Chapter 3

The Workings of Human Reincarnation

3-1 The Spirit Realm

Every time we finish a pass through this world for a lifetime of practice and then atonement in the Astral Realm, we return to the Spirit Realm (the home and origin of the human soul), and spend a period there much longer than our lives in this world.

So what is it like in the Spirit Realm, and what kind of a place is it? In this section I would like to describe the Spirit Realm.

A look at the Spirit Realm

The Spirit Realm is a far better place than this world. The climate in the Spirit Realm is incredibly comfortable, neither hot nor cold, and feels something like a bright day in May. Nature exists, as in this world—mountains, rivers, plants, and so on. But since it's not polluted like much of the world in the Present Realm, the air is clear, the water is pure, and everything in nature is beautiful. There are animals there too, but they dwell in their natural state, and aren't kept as pets as they are in this world. Because the same sun and moon exist both in the Spirit Realm and in this world, there is day and night there too. People live together in houses as families of up to five people, and they eat two meals a day (lunch and dinner). The big dif-

Chapter 3 The Workings of Human Reincarnation

ference between life there and life in the material world is that, in the Spirit Realm, people encounter deities on a regular basis in the course of their daily life. They can be seen by people of the Spirit Realm, and give them direct guidance. We could say that the Spirit Realm is a place where humans and deities exist together.

The civilization of the Spirit Realm is far more advanced than that of the material world. People drive cars in the Spirit Realm, but they are similar to environmentally friendly "clean" cars. They also have television (but no commercials), airplanes, helicopters, and other forms of transportation. Speaking of vehicles, once in a while here in the Present Realm, there is a commotion in the mass media about "UFO sightings." UFOs take many forms, from disc shapes to airplane-like constructions, but the truth about UFOs is that they are the vehicles of the inhabitants of the Spirit Realm, moving freely in four-dimensional space. Again, because the four-dimensional Spirit Realm and the three-dimensional Present Realm overlap and influence each other, on rare occasions these vehicles can be seen in this world too.

On Auras

Have you ever heard of an *aura* before?

● **Auras**

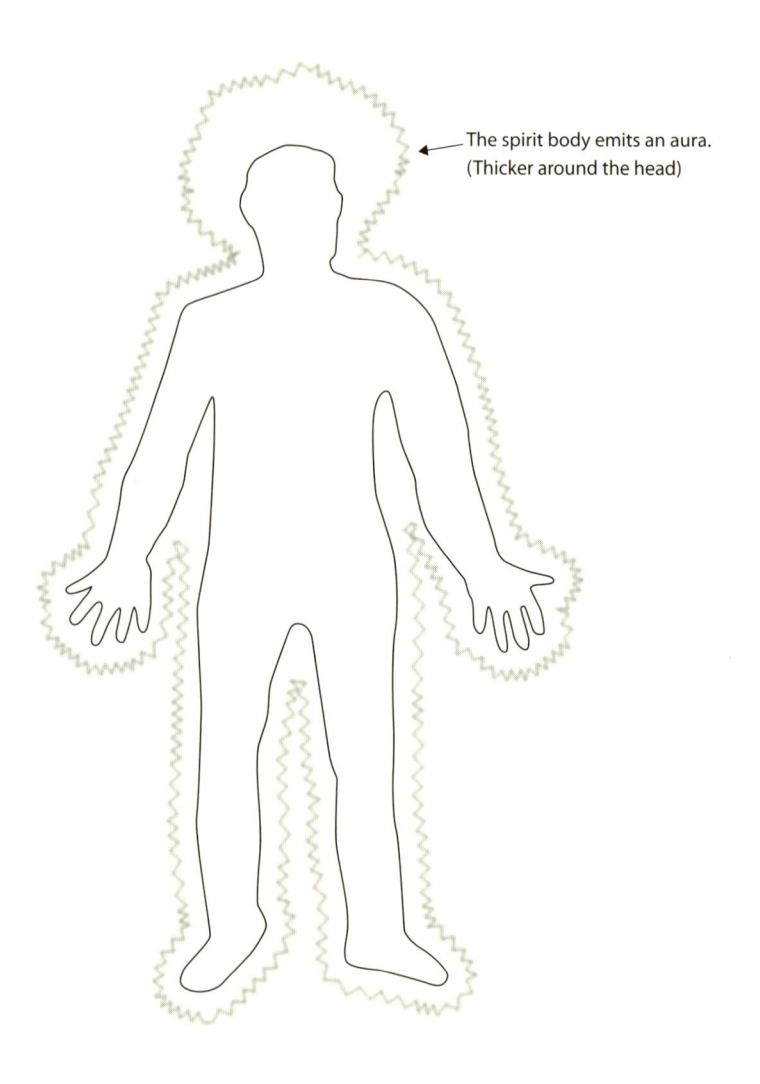

The spirit body emits an aura.
(Thicker around the head)

● Aura colors and thickness

Spirit phase	Lowest ⟶ Highest
Aura colors	Black (muddy), Dark gray, Gray, Greenish, Blue, Purple

Number of lives led	10	20	25	30
Aura thickness	About 5 cm (2 in.)	About 15 cm (6 in.)	About 50 cm (20 in.)	About 100 cm (40 in.)

Auras are like flames exuded from our spirit bodies. They are invisible to the human eye in the Present Realm, but when we return to the Spirit Realm they become visible again. The thickness and color of an aura indicates the *spirit phase* (the level of their soul). The thicker and more beautiful the aura, the higher the spirit phase of that person.

In general, a person's spirit phase is proportional to the number of times that they have lived in the Present Realm. Which means that the more lives they have lead in practice in this world, the more cultivated their souls are, and their spirit phase is said to be higher.

In the Present Realm, we normally determine hierarchy based on age (judging by looks and fitness). In the Spirit Realm, however, people do not age, retaining their youth of a 20-year-old. So they don't judge based on the appearance of the spirit body itself. They judge, rather, by the spirit phase based on the color and thickness of the aura their spirit body emanates.

Divine communism in the Spirit Realm

Fundamentally, people in the Spirit Realm live and work (men outside the home, and women in the home) alongside people with a spirit phase on the same level. As such, the Spirit Realm is a society which is clearly divided into classes based on differences in spirit phase.

Here deities serve as politicians, running a communist government, and they guide the people of the Spirit Realm in everything they do (this arrangement is called divine communism). Deities treat all of the people of the Spirit Realm fairly, and needless to say there is no scandal or corruption as there is among the politicians of this world. Further, in this communist system, the wages are all equal, which eliminates various differences that we find in the material world.

In addition, because everyone living in the Spirit Realm is a member of the yellow race, there is no racism as there often is in the Present Realm. In this kind of society, there is no one who sullies their hands with crime, and there are no police stations or prisons. Of course, since spirit bodies are immune to illness and injury, there are no hospitals, either. Everyone in the Spirit Realm can relax in true ease, and lead happy and fun lives. This is truly heaven.

3-2 A general overview of reincarnation and transmigration

In this section, I will explain how human souls are originally created in the Spirit Realm, and provide a basic overview of how our souls are cultivated by repeating the processes of reincarnation and transmigration. In Sections 3-3 to 3-7, we'll look at each step in more detail.

Birth in the Spirit Realm

Even in the Spirit Realm, men and women get married (by permission of God). When they get married, they get a house of their own. Then, the woman gets pregnant. (There is no infertility in the Spirit Realm.) Just the same as in the material world, children begin life in the Spirit Realm in their mothers' wombs. God creates a new soul for the child, and place it into the pineal gland around the 16th to 19th week of pregnancy. Then, after about 40 weeks, the child is born as a baby. Thereafter, the child's spirit body grows quickly, and, after completing the compulsory education (10 years) of the Spirit Realm, they are fully grown at the age of 20.[6] After that, their spirit body no longer matures, or ages.

You with this book in your hand, whether you remember it or not, you were also born in the Spirit Realm, your true home, and raised by your parents there long, long ago. Your parents in the Spirit Realm are basically different from those in the Present Realm. Your parents in the Present Realm are temporary, but your true parents are in the Spirit Realm, and are always watching over you.

[6] The 10 years of compulsory education in the Spirit Realm is comparable to elementary and junior high schools in this world. There are no schools equivalent to high school or university in the Spirit Realm.

Birth in the Present Realm

Our souls can never improve if we live only in the Spirit Realm. Human souls can only be improved by cultivating them through life practice in the material world. That's why a fully matured soul and spirit body, which was born and raised by parents in the Spirit Realm, make its first voyage to the Present Realm being seen off by its parents.

Life in the Present Realm

We are born into all sorts of different circumstances and environments in this world. There are those who are born to poor households, and those who are born to the richest. We are also born into one of many races. We are all inspired and challenged by circumstances we have been given for the practice of life.

In the material world, auras, and thus differences in spirit phase, cannot be seen, and people of completely different spirit phases come together to form one society. People's values and ways of thinking can be completely different depending on their spirit phase. There are those who only seek money and objects, there are those who care nothing for others, and there are those who kindly give consideration to others. With all the different types of people living in the same society, tensions will naturally occur. Discord among races sometimes happens on a global scale.

We all live our daily lives in the middle of all this discord we can't experience in the Spirit Realm. We experience all the pain, hardship, pleasure, happiness, beauty, and love. And, by working hard to live in harmony with all of these things, our souls are cultivated.

Back to the Spirit Realm

Unfortunately though, many people commit sins in the course of their life practice, and are made to pay for it after death in the Astral Realm. When the atonement is completed, the soul is allowed to return to the Spirit Realm. Some individuals, however, may even fall into a hell called the Beast Hell when they die, and, instead of returning to the Spirit Realm after their time there, they are forced to be born again as animals in the material world (transmigration).

Repetition of this cycle

If we were to just stay in the Spirit Realm enjoying ourselves, our souls would not improve. This is why we are reborn into the Present Realm (reincarnation). God makes us reincarnate over and over.

We are currently in the middle of this process. How many lives have you already had up to now?

You can't tell now, but will find out after you die, when you complete your atonement in the Astral Realm and return to the Spirit Realm.

The product of this repetition

Why, then, do we have to continue to cultivate our souls through repeating this cycle or reincarnation?

That's because humans can go to the Realm of Deity and

Chapter 3 The Workings of Human Reincarnation

● A general overview of reincarnation and transmigration

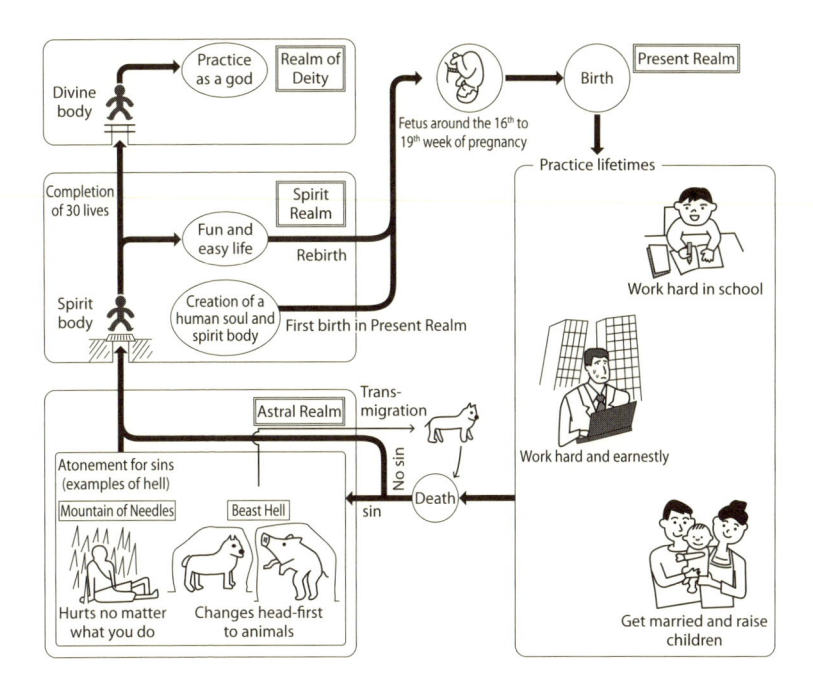

[Diagram showing the cycle of reincarnation: Divine body → Practice as a god (Realm of Deity) → Fetus around the 16th to 19th week of pregnancy → Birth (Present Realm) → Practice lifetimes (Work hard in school, Work hard and earnestly, Get married and raise children) → Death → either "No sin" path to Astral Realm (Transmigration) or "sin" path to Atonement for sins (examples of hell): Mountain of Needles (Hurts no matter what you do), Beast Hell (Changes head-first to animals) → Spirit body → Creation of a human soul and spirit body (First birth in Present Realm) / Fun and easy life (Spirit Realm, Rebirth) → Completion of 30 lives → back to Divine body]

become gods. That is to say, we are all cultivating and purifying our souls over and over for our greater goal of becoming gods. More specifically, after 30 lives of practice in the Present Realm, humans can become gods (the 30 lives do not include transmigrated lives). Characteristics of souls vary among different individuals. Some souls commit few sins in each life even though they are born fewer times for life practice in the material world. In contrast, some commit great amounts of sin in each life even

51

if they are reborn many, many times.

Around the time the number of lives practiced reaches 25, however, most of the personal differences are eliminated, and the soul improves towards not committing sins. After a human soul completes its 30th practice life, it becomes a god soul.

I'm sure that there are many among my readers who have believed that there is just one God. Indeed, there is just one Almighty Creator who made all life and all material things.[7] That God occupies the highest position in the upper level of the seven-dimensional Realm of Deity, and controls everything in the universe. (The Creator did not rise up from a human soul, but has existed since the beginning as God.)

There are, however, many other deities aside from this "God". To begin with, there are 10 original gods along with the Creator, who did not ascend from humanity. (These original deities are called *Amatsukami*.) There are a great number of other gods that have ascended from human being in the way I described.

Gods and 10 original gods have the appearance of the yellow race. This is the same appearance of the true form (spirit body) shared by all of humanity. We are made in such a way so

Chapter 3 The Workings of Human Reincarnation

● **Hierarchy of the Realm of Deity**

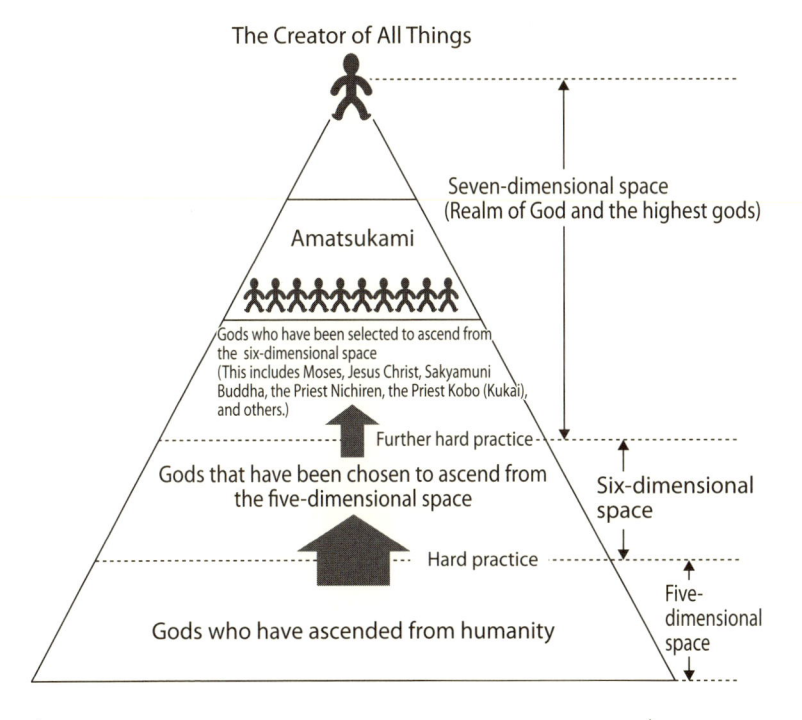

The Creator of All Things

Amatsukami

Gods who have been selected to ascend from the six-dimensional space
(This includes Moses, Jesus Christ, Sakyamuni Buddha, the Priest Nichiren, the Priest Kobo (Kukai), and others.)

Seven-dimensional space (Realm of God and the highest gods)

Further hard practice

Gods that have been chosen to ascend from the five-dimensional space

Six-dimensional space

Hard practice

Gods who have ascended from humanity

Five-dimensional space

(The 10 Amatsukami maintain and manage the universe in accordance with the will of the Almighty Creator, giving orders and directions to other deities stationed all throughout the universe.)

that we will eventually be able to be made like gods. When we ascend to divinity, our spirit bodies are called divine bodies. Souls that have just attained divinity are initially stationed in the five-dimensional Realm of Deity. Even after becoming gods, they must face severe challenges and work hard in their practice in order to ascend to six-dimensional and then seven-dimensional space (the highest level of the Realm of Deity). To give just a few examples of those who have ascended to the seven-dimensional space as gods, we can point to Moses, Jesus Christ, Sakyamuni Buddha, the Priest Nichiren, the Priest Kobo (Kukai).

[7] The Gods prayed to by people of various religions around the world (Amaterasu, Iyasaka, Vairocana, Amitabha Tathagata, Brahma, Yahweh, Jehovah, Allah, and so on) are in actuality different expressions of the one Almighty Creator.

3-3 How we are born into the Present Realm

In this section, I would like to tell you the story of how we come from the Spirit Realm to be born in the Present Realm. You are the main character in the story. Have some fun imagining yourself going through this.

....

You have already been born into a life of practice in the material world a number of times. In your previous life, you were a samurai in Japan's Kamakura period, over 700 years ago.[8] After that, you completed your atonement in the Astral Realm, and it has already been some time now since you returned to the Spirit Realm.

Chapter 3 *The Workings of Human Reincarnation*

"Seems to be getting about time to go get born in the Present Realm again ..."

"Just staying here in the Spirit Realm for much longer won't improve my spirit phase ..."

While you're having thoughts like this one day, messengers from deities will call on you.

"Get ready for some more practice in the Present Realm!"

Once it's decided that you're to be reborn again in the Present Realm, a rebirth party will be held in your honor.[9] This is something similar to a farewell party.

You'll be sent off with words of encouragement from all around, like "Go get'em!" "Don't do anything bad so you don't have to go to hell this time!" and "Fix all those bad habits!"

How bad of a person could you have been in your previous life? At your rebirth party, everyone is there to encourage you to lead a correct life this time.

Then, when there is about a week left before you are to make your descent to the Present Realm, you go to the waiting area. In the waiting area, there are lots of others who are, like you, also planning to descend to the material world. At the waiting area, you will learn more or less what kind of life you will lead this time, including things like what sort of household you will be born into and who you will marry later. This is how you're going to get yourself in the right frame of mind for being born this time. You may be surprised to learn that the courses of human lives are, to a certain extent, determined from the very beginning.

Then, when your mother in the Present Realm is around the 16th to 19th week of her pregnancy, your soul and spirit body descend and enter the physical body of the fetus, after waiting in the waiting area. When your soul and spirit body enter a physical body, an astral body exactly the same as your physical body is created. This is exactly the point when your spirit body, which has the youth of a 20-year-old, and your physical and astral bodies in the form of a baby, are completely formed.

Furthermore, souls and spirit bodies do have an original gender. But this doesn't mean that only boys are born into the bodies of boys in the Present Realm just because they have souls and spirit bodies of boys, and the same applies to girls. In our repeated practice lives, we are made to experience being both a man and a woman. What, then, is your true gender? You

Chapter 3 The Workings of Human Reincarnation

can't know that for sure until you return to the Spirit Realm once again.

Up to now I've described the process that the soul goes through, as it leaves the Spirit Realm with the spirit body, to the Present Realm to enter the physical body of a fetus. But you probably have absolutely no memory of this happening. The reason for this is that, in the period between the time our soul and spirit body enter a physical body around the 16th to 19th week of pregnancy, and the time we are born at the end of pregnancy, deities erase all of our memory.[10] If we were to have this memory while in the Present Realm, it wouldn't be much practice for us. It is important for the improvement of our souls to avoid committing sins and to discipline ourselves so as not to repeat the errors of past lives, even under the circumstances of our memory being completely erased and starting from zero.

Then, as the end of the pregnancy nears, you are born from your mother into the world as a child. While you are unable to see them, right when you are born, the five spirits known as your "watcher spirits" will assemble around you, and begin their watch over you. These watcher spirits will be watching you intently your entire life.[11]

● **Watcher spirits**

Most watcher spirits are men and your ancestors sent from the Spirit Realm. They wear variety of clothes such as kimono and western clothing.

These watcher spirits are sometimes mistaken for protective spirits or guardian deities, but normally, they are not attendant upon humans. The role of these watcher spirits is essentially to monitor and record that person's entire life. They accurately record that person's words, deeds, personality, and ideas. However, in rare cases, when the person's spirit level is fairly high, the spirits do sometimes protect and guide.

....

You have come through the process described above, and

you have succeeded in being born into the Present Realm. From there, you have come to experience a great variety of things in this material world.

[8] The eras in which we have lived and the occupations we have held in our past lives are different for everyone.
[9] Only before our first life is the celebration called a first birthday party.
[10] Some children have a memory of being in the womb for a short period of time after they are born. This is called fetal memory. As children grow older, however, it is eventually lost and forgotten.
[11] Sometimes there is a change in a person's line-up of watcher spirits. Particularly, for a woman who changes her last name when she marries, her husband's ancestors may take over as her watcher spirits.

3-4 The significance of birth in this world

Let's take a moment here to think about the significance of being born as humans into the Present Realm (this world).

As I have already stated more than once, we as humans are born into the Present Realm in order that we may practice living and cultivate our souls and minds. To put it another way, this world is a place of learning and practice for the soul, and it is not a place to pursue nothing but money and objects, to seek only to satisfy our own desires, and to gain status and honor.

So what does this "life practice" exactly entail?

"Practice" might sound a little overblown. When we say "practice" in the spiritual sense, images of monks in seated meditation or waterfall meditation for hours and hours on end, living in austerity and hardship for spiritual benefits, may be the first to come to mind. But this sort of discipline and austerity only puts a strain on the body, and does nothing for cultivating the soul. "Life practice" is not that kind of specialized religious or spiritual practice, but instead simply living correctly as a person in all of the various circumstances we are given. This is the only kind of practice by which the human soul can be cultivated.

For students, for example, simply going to school and taking it seriously are forms of this practice. They have to mind the rules, and study hard. But human minds don't grow just by studying. Getting along with friends and others at school, doing as told by parents, and helping out around the house are all forms of practice.

When we leave school, finding the right job for the world and for people, and then working earnestly, is also a form of practice. Still, if we work hard and shed blood and tears for a job that is not the right one for us, our souls are polluted rather than being cultivated.

Also, even if you have the right job, but work only to make money, your soul will be polluted by it. That means that a job is not for the benefit of gaining status or glory, or even for getting by. It's what you do for the world and for others. It can be difficult at times to work for the world and for others, but you will learn from experience, and your strife will become the very thing by which your soul is cultivated.

In summary, life practice means properly doing all the things we are supposed to do, and living with a spirit of altruism which makes us devote ourselves to others.

And please remember that, as explained in the previous section, we all have watcher spirits who monitor and record our entire lives in detail. We as humans have a tendency to sin in ways big and small, thinking it will be OK if "no one is looking" or if it's "only a little bit." But the fact is that all of this is recorded by these watcher spirits. These records will be the basis upon which deities judge where you will go after you die. In the Present Realm, even if you were to sin, if there is no one there to witness it, no one will blame you for it. But God and other deities know about everything through the records of these watcher spirits. This is why it's so important to live earnestly and righteously as a person, whether anyone is watching you or not.

There are many who marry at the right age. Marriage is the biggest practice of all. This is because there is nothing better we can do as humans to cultivate our souls than to live together under one roof with a man or woman who was born and raised in completely different environments.

While you're in love, you may only be showing the good of yourselves to each other. But when you get married, you begin to see the reality. You'll start to notice little things that catch and annoy, like the kinds of food they like or their living habits.

This gets even more difficult when you have children. Children don't grow up just the way their parents want them to. The opinions of husband and wife on the children's education can be divided, and children go through their rebellious phases. Child-rearing means becoming responsible for a soul that is still in the process of its growth, and this is a huge opportunity for practice given us by God and other deities. Building relationships of love, patience, and consideration between spouses and their children to create a harmonious household cultivates our souls.

As a general rule, all people that are born must marry. If for example, you are given the opportunity to marry, but end up spending your life alone by your continued refusal of marriage, God and other deities will judge this to be a sin, as they regard this as your throwing away the practice of marriage.

Some people would say that no matter how much they want to get married, they can't. As I explained in the previous section, the courses of human lives are to a certain extent determined from the beginning, and the person with whom you marry is also decided (see the column "Your destined soul mate").

For certain people, however, there are reasons (sins from a past life, for example) that prevent God and other deities from permitting them to be married. It's not necessarily true that those who have gone their whole lives without marrying have committed any sin.

We were born to go through this kind of life practice in this world in order to cultivate our souls. All of the worries and pain that appear in our lives have in a sense been given to us by God and other deities for our own betterment. This is why there are so many people who, looking back on their lives, find that their worries and troubles have outweighed the fun and the happy times. God and other deities are watching for how you will approach, and get over these troubles when faced with them. It is through this process that human souls can be cultivated and made to grow.

> **Column: Your destined soul mate**
>
> Deities explain to us our fate in this life in the waiting area before we descend to the Present Realm. This includes who your spouse (your destined soul mate) will be.
>
> Many of my readers may be thinking this is ridiculous, because you think that you met your partner by chance, and got married because you fell in love.
>
> But that is all according to God's plan. Though it may be difficult to understand, you met and came to love your partner because deities gently guided you in that direction using your watcher spirits. Nevertheless, in rare cases, people do sometimes marry someone other than who they were supposed to.
>
> Basically, your marriage partner changes every time you repeat the reincarnation cycle. That is to say, you don't always marry the same person (soul). There are those, however, who do marry the same partner even

after being reborn. This happens when married life between the partners did not go well. For couples that quarrel constantly and don't even make an effort to get along with each other, deities make them practice marrying the same person over and over again each time they are born. When the two are finally able to live a married life and get along, that practice will be completed, and the two will not marry each other again.

If you don't like the husband (or wife) you have now, and you don't want to spend the next life stuck with him/her too, then try to make an effort to get along in your married life for the rest of the time in this life.

And remember to think of marriage as the greatest "life practice".

3-5 Leaving the Present Realm

After we are born into this world and complete a certain amount of life practice, we once again return to the other side. This is the "death" of the Present Realm. No matter how far we advance medically and scientifically, we will absolutely never be able to evade death. This is an absolute truth.

So how do we go about departing this world?

Here I will go into in some detail about what it is like in the instant we find ourselves facing death, and what happens after we die.[12] This is something that will undoubtedly happen to you too. So imagine yourself going through this.

[12] This section assumes death under normal conditions, such as aging or disease. For information on what happens to those who die by suicide, homicide, or accident (unnatural death), see Section 3-9.

A dream of crossing the River Styx

Right before they die, everyone falls into a so-called unconscious state. In this state, they all have a dream (or hallucination) of crossing the River Styx.

I'm sure that many of my readers have heard of the River Styx—the river that divides this world and the next. This river does not exist in reality, but is merely an image that appears in the dream shown to those in an unconscious state just before they die. Everyone who dies, regardless of how they died, be it old age, disease, suicide, a sudden accident, or whatever, is shown this dream by deities, as a device to communicate to the individual that they are in fact dead.

● The River Styx

In the dream, there is a river and a pier. The river is roughly 100 meters (about 110 yards) across, and its water flows slowly from right to left. If you walk out onto the pier, you will find a small boat tied up, and there will be a boatman there. On the far bank, beautifully colored meadows full of flowers can be seen, and you will feel very confident in your desire to get on the boat and go there.

When you get into the boat, the boatman will slowly push off to take you across the river. When you get out on the other side, the meadows of flowers vanish all at once. That is the exact instant that your physical heart stops (this is called "cardiac death"). This is the moment where we shed our physical bodies and leave this world (three-dimensional space) for the next one (four-dimensional space). Thereafter, you use your astral body (which means you become a ghost).

Occasionally, instead of reaching the other side of the River Styx in their dream, people stop and come back to consciousness in the middle of the dream, and "come back to life." Often, people with a near-death experience have described seeing beautiful scenery where they could see "many lovely flowers blooming" when they were unconscious. These people woke up and returned to life without crossing the River Styx.

After death, the spirit cord

Those who cross the river wake up from the dream, and notice that their own physical body is just about 60 centimeters (about 2 feet) below them. Faced with this reality, many of the dead become startled and start to panic.[13]

After that, the family of the deceased will start to notice changes in the physical body (now a corpse). The family may be calling desperately to the remains. The deceased and their family are right next to each other, but the spaces they inhabit have different dimensions. The deceased in four-dimensional space is able to see and hear their family in three-dimensional

Chapter 3 The Workings of Human Reincarnation

space, but the family in three-dimensional space cannot see the deceased person, now an astral body in four-dimensional space, nor can they hear the voice of the departed.

In this way, the deceased is made aware of their own death by crossing the river, seeing their own physical body as a corpse lain out in front of their own eyes, and seeing the reactions of their family towards their remains. They will be clearly aware of the fact that it's not over when we die.

When you die, four of the five watcher spirits that have been monitoring your entire life will return to the Spirit Realm. The one remaining watcher spirit will then be made visible to the deceased, and will guide and take care of the deceased thereafter. Then, the family and relatives of the deceased person in the Spirit Realm will come to meet them.

So what happens to the deceased floating above their physical body?

In actual fact, the astral body of a deceased person, for a short while after their death, is attached to the person's physical body, which is connected by an invisible cord, called a spirit cord, stretching from the back of the head of the astral body to that of the physical body, meaning the astral body is unable to

- **The physical body (the remains) and astral body immediately after cardiac death**

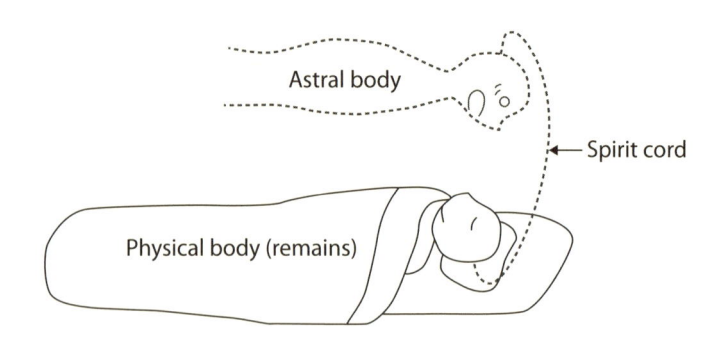

Astral body

Spirit cord

Physical body (remains)

move freely apart from its physical body (now dead).

In addition, when the physical body is harmed in this state, the astral body is also exposed to this harm through the spirit cord, and the deceased feels pain. This is why we must not harm the remains of the deceased by doing autopsies or dissections, or harvesting organs.

[13] One watcher spirit will take care of you, but this watcher spirit won't reason with, or try to comfort, the deceased. So the deceased will have a sense of anxiety about what will happen next.

Problems with vigils and funerals

After that, a vigil, funeral, and other rites will be held for the deceased. At these events, the friends, family, and acquaintances of the deceased person line up to pay their respects and mourn the loss.[14] The deceased watches these mourners from the position just about 60 centimeters (about 2 feet) above the coffin. There are a few things that cause big problems for the deceased when it comes to vigils and funerals. We'll address just two of these.

[14] Funerals are a graduation ceremony for life, so in actuality they should be a celebratory event.

● **Dry ice**

The dry ice, which sometimes placed in the coffin with the deceased to prevent corruption of the remains, freezes the deceased person. As touched upon earlier, for a time after death the physical body and the astral body are connected by the spirit cord, and any damage to the physical body affects the astral body as well. When a corpse is put on dry ice, the astral body of the individual is also frozen, and the deceased feels the pain of this freezing. This is why it's much better not to use dry ice for this purpose.

● **Burning incense**

The smoke of incense is also something very trying for the deceased. When the physical body has been shed, the senses of the deceased are much sharper than they were in life. The sense of smell in particular will be about 10 times more sensitive. That's why the deceased person can't stand the smoke.

Incense began as something to get rid of the odor of corruption from corpses, used by survivors.[15] But because there is something about incense that gives things sort of a mystical air, people tend to mistake this for some kind of offering for the deceased, as the custom has become today. There is no fragrance that will save you from death. The scents are only scents, and for the deceased, it's just smoky.

So in this way, the deceased suffers the horrible cold and smokiness while they watch the vigil and the funeral from above their coffin. They are happy, though, that so many relatives and friends came to say goodbye.

---

[15] If you simply want to get rid of the odor of the corpse, try placing flowers around the remains, rather than burning incense.

The spirit cord: cremation and true death

The event that the deceased person is waiting for after the funeral is cremation or burial. The deceased must be dreadfully frightened when their physical body is placed into a cremation furnace.

Chapter 3 The Workings of Human Reincarnation

"Hey, I'm still up here above my body!"
"Are you trying to burn me alive, or what?!"

It may seem strange that someone already dead should be afraid of being burned to death, but it's not that far-fetched if you think about it this way: even though they're dead, the deceased still have the same consciousness, and the same senses they had when alive. It's no wonder that they should be afraid that their physical body is going to be burned up.

But please don't worry. The spirit cord that connects the astral body to the physical body is snapped just before the flames engulf the corpse in the furnace. It is a well-known fact among the workers at crematoriums that, just before a body is burned, the torso rises up. That is the precise moment that the spirit cord that connects the astral body and the physical body snaps.[16] In cases of burial rather than cremation, the spirit cord snaps when the coffin is placed into the ground, and the dirt on top of the coffin becomes level. Even when a body is left and neither cremated nor buried, the spirit cord is made to snap within about a week's time at the longest.

This snapping of the spirit cord is "true death." After true death, the deceased person is free to move about. Though the deceased is now free to move around, the cremation being over, an indescribable feeling overwhelms them at seeing their own physical body reduced to ashes and bones.[17] After that, though they can't be seen, they go home with their families.

[16] Those who were very stubborn and attached to their lives have a tough time breaking the spirit cord, and rise up a number of times.
[17] The weight of the deceased without their body (that is, an astral body) is about 30 grams (about 1 ounce).

Altars, memorial tablets, and offerings

The deceased who have returned home sometimes go other places, but normally they are in their altar space, about 60 centimeters (about 2 feet) above their memorial tablet, lying with their head to the north. The clothes they are wearing are the same as those they were wearing when placed in their coffin. They take one meal every day.

You may think it's really odd for someone without a physical body to need food. Even when we die, though, we still have the same senses that we had when alive, so we do get hungry. Of course, the deceased, having no physical body, can't take the food into their hand directly to eat it, but they are able to gain a feeling of fullness when they breathe in the steam and smell of the offerings.

Chapter 3 The Workings of Human Reincarnation

● **The deceased at home**
(Give offerings that are warm so that they produce steam and a smell.)

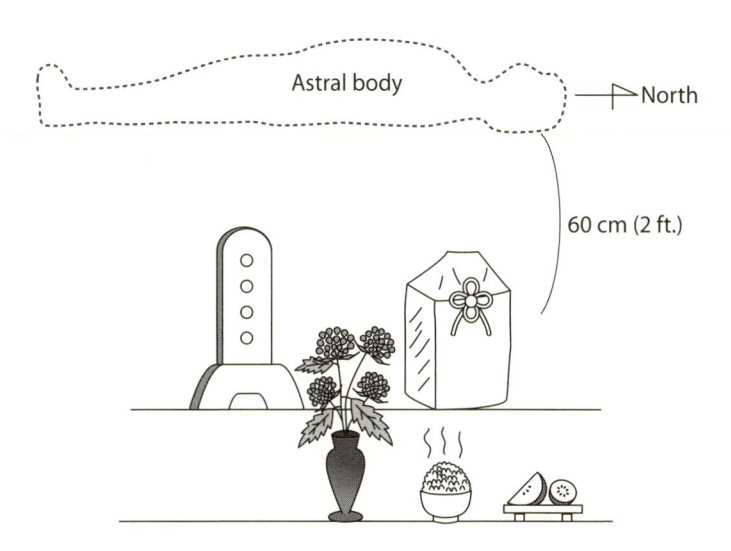

Astral body — North

60 cm (2 ft.)

Further, because the deceased do go out sometimes, let them know at about what time you will put out the offering by facing a spot about 60 centimeters (about 2 feet) above the altar and saying what time the meal will be prepared.

3-6 The true significance of the 49-day period and divine judgment

In Buddhist traditions, when someone in the family dies,

there is first a vigil, a funeral, then memorial services held on the 7th day after death, on the 14th day after death, and so forth, and the services concerning mourning are graduated. The service held on the 49th day after death is the final step of the services, commonly known as the "end of mourning." As such, the 49th-day service is an important marker in the Buddhist memorial services, but why is it 49 days? What is the real significance of these 49 days?

The true significance of the 49-day period

After the deceased has been cremated and gone back home, though they cannot be seen, they are staying in their own home in the Present Realm for a period of 49 days. On the 49th day, the deceased goes to the court of Deity in the Astral Realm, and is evaluated in what is termed *divine judgment*. This divine judgment determines where the deceased will go next.

So why do God and other deities keep the deceased waiting in the Present Realm for 49 days after death?

There are profound reasons for this. I will explain three of them below.

(1) To remove attachments to the Present Realm
First of all, this period is for the deceased to get rid of their

Chapter 3 The Workings of Human Reincarnation

attachments to this world (the Present Realm) and prepare themselves for the journey to the other side. Everyone is attached to this world to greater or lesser degrees when they die. We all have our various reasons, whether it's being worried about a wife and a child left behind, or some work that has been left undone. Still, the deceased is dead after all and will have to get rid of these attachments. No one can stay caught up in this world forever. Thus, God and other deities provide the 49 days for us as a period of preparation for crossing over to the other side, and thereby remove our attachment to this world.

(2) To look back on one's life and to reflect upon sins and impurities

At the time of the divine judgment conducted on the 49th day, the words and deeds, personality, and ideas of the deceased are judged. Many people sin in the course of their lives. It is desirable that we should, as much as possible, be aware of our own sins, and reflect upon them while we are still alive. But there are few chances in life to look back and reflect this way.

God and other deities give the deceased an opportunity to look back on their life and repent of sins and impurities. This is what the 49 days are provided for. For that reason, the one remaining watcher spirit also records this extremely important 49-day period after death in addition to the life of the person.

The result of the divine judgment, and thus your destination in the afterlife could change a great deal depending on your reflecting and looking back during this period.

The families that are left behind should also use this time to help the deceased reflect on their life. You can face a spot about 60 centimeters (about 2 feet) above the altar in your home, and talk about the good and bad points of the deceased. For example, say your grandfather, who was somewhat stubborn in this life, has passed away. You could encourage him with words from your heart, saying, "You know you could be a little stubborn sometimes. Maybe you had better rethink that."

It might also be good if you spoke to them about what will happen to them next (the significance of the 49 days; that there will be a divine judgment; that, if they are found to have sinned, they will be sent to the Astral Realm; that, if they repent, they will be able to return to the Spirit Realm; and so on). Just as when they were alive, even after death, it's quite hard to reflect honestly on their own actions. However, by hearing the words of their family, it becomes somewhat easier for the deceased to understand.

(3) Stepping out for last goodbyes

The deceased person stays in their house for the 49-day

Chapter 3 The Workings of Human Reincarnation

period, but they also go out of the house and meet with friends and relatives. They go to say their final goodbyes. This 49-day period is also used for this: by saying goodbye, the deceased is able to get their heart and mind in order, and prepare themselves for the other side. The deceased walk just as living people do, and they use various modes of transportation, including buses and trains, to get around.[18] As astral bodies are able to pass through materials in three-dimensional space (buildings, walls, etc.), the deceased can slip onto the train easily even if the gate and the doors are closed. (They ride for free!) If we could see four-dimensional space, you can be sure that you would see that the bullet trains are full of spirits out to say their last goodbyes.

---

[18] There are those who, when they die, can move about from place to place instantaneously (basically, these are people whose spirit phases are high).

Divine judgment

On the 49th day after death, the one remaining watcher spirit has the deceased remove the clothing they have been wearing since they were placed in their coffin, and they are made to wear a simple white kimono-like outfit with short sleeves and knee length. (The outfit should be wrapped around the body with the left side over the right side, signifying death, and it is tied with a string). Then the watcher spirit will take the deceased person to the court of Deity in the Astral Realm.[19] Court is in session every day. All of the deceased who died 49 days ago on that day are lined up and waiting in the chamber, all wearing matching white outfits and accompanied by each person's watcher spirit.

Then, when they are summoned in turns, they go to stand in front of the desk of a judge (a god in seven-dimensional space).[20] At this time, the watcher will stand behind the deceased on the left, and read out the records of the person's life and their 49 days since death. Watcher spirits never lie in their reports, so there is no chance for an appeal (and of course there are no prosecutors or lawyers either). After hearing the end of the report by the watcher spirit, the judge promptly makes a final ruling according to the laws of the universe (divine rule) and hands down the decision. In this way, it is decided where the deceased will go.

Unfortunately, as we go through this life practice in the material world, we commit sins to a greater or lesser extent. Many must go to the Astral Realm after this divine judgment in order to atone for those sins. If the deceased person escapes, saying that they don't want to go to the Astral Realm, the watcher spirit simply let them go. That individual, however, becomes a wandering spirit in the Present Realm, lost and unable to return to the Spirit Realm.

When people have been reincarnated close to 30 times, their human soul approaches the level of a god soul, and seldom commit sins. These people do not atone for anything in the Astral Realm, and are allowed to return to the Spirit Realm, the home and origin of the human soul, directly.

[19] The Astral Realm is divided up by country, and there is one divine court for each country.
[20] In Buddhism, the god who hands down judgments is called Enma, and is known for his fearsome image. But the actual judges (gods in seven-dimensional space) don't have frightening appearances.

3-7 Atonement in the Astral Realm, and then to the Spirit Realm

The levels of the Astral Realm

What happens next to the deceased who go to the Astral Realm after their 49 days and divine judgment?

Depending on the nature and severity of their sins, the deceased will be sent to various levels in the Astral Realm. Then begins your life of painful atonement at your assigned level. By atoning through pain for the sins of their previous life, and

● The levels in the Astral Realm

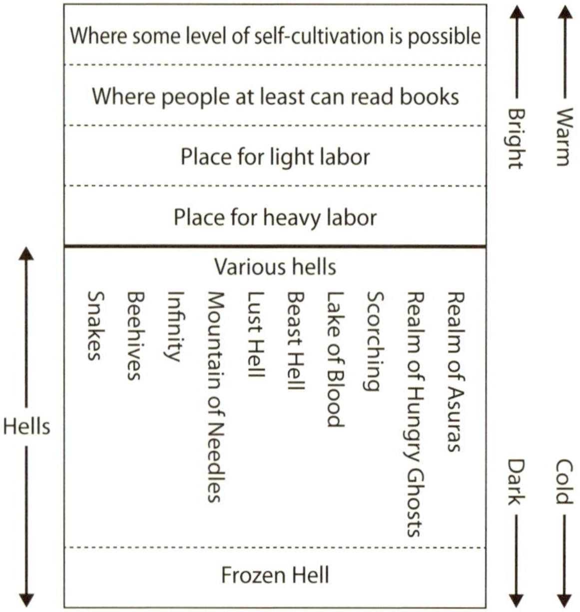
Where some level of self-cultivation is possible
Where people at least can read books
Place for light labor
Place for heavy labor
Various hells
Realm of Asuras
Realm of Hungry Ghosts
Scorching
Lake of Blood
Beast Hell
Lust Hell
Mountain of Needles
Infinity
Beehives
Snakes
Frozen Hell
Hells
Bright
Dark
Warm
Cold

removing attachments to the Present Realm, the dead can ascend the levels in the Astral Realm.

The Astral Realm is divided into six levels. The upper four levels are for atonement outside of hell. The lower two are hells. The further down you go in the hells, the darker and deeper the suffering for atonement is.

Chapter 3 The Workings of Human Reincarnation

● The Frozen Hell

83

Atonement in the Astral Realm

Let's begin with the very lowest of the levels of hell—the "Frozen Hell." As its name suggests, this hell is as cold and dark as a place can get. The people cast into this hell are frozen stiff and solid. Even under this tragic state, they must reflect upon their own sins.

What kinds of sins are categorized into this hell?

One example that may be somewhat unexpected is suicides.[21] Deities consider suicide to be an abandonment of the life practice given to you by them, and so it is regarded as a serious sin. Suicide is an extremely important issue, which will be addressed in more detail in Section 3-9.

There are 10 different kinds of hells in the upper level of the Frozen Hell, namely, the Realm of Asuras, the Realm of Hungry Ghosts, Scorching, Lake of Blood, Beast Hell, Lust Hell, Mountain of Needles, Infinity, Beehives, and Snakes. Whichever hell they are cast into, the deceased must atone for their sins amidst great suffering.

Not only great sins for which one would be punished in the Present Realm by prison (such as, murder, robbery), but also bad words and deeds, or even just bad traits or ideas regarded as sins by deities, can land a person in a hell according to the

Chapter 3 The Workings of Human Reincarnation

● The Realm of Hungry Ghosts

85

severity of the sin.

According to the laws of the universe (divine rule), people who committed specific sins, including those who "were vindictive," "always complained," "spoke badly of others," "were deceitful," "were selfish," "caused trouble for others," and "were wasters," go to predetermined hell as sinners. In particular, those who "were selfish," "caused trouble for others," or "were wasters" are cast into the Realm of Hungry Ghosts.[22]

A specific example of someone who "caused trouble for others" and has been sent to this hell is a smoker. My readers may be surprised to hear that one can be sent to hell for something like smoking. Smoking not only damages the body of the smoker, but also causes trouble for everyone around. For this reason, deities judge even smoking to be a sin that falls into the category of causing trouble for others. Thus they punish people for it after death. It is said that the Realm of Hungry Ghosts has the largest number of people, and that it is the sins we are most familiar with that could land us there. That's why I would like to spend just a little space talking about this hell in detail.

In this hell, everyone is placed in individual caves. There, as they are constantly hungry, they cry out for food. Even when they find food, the instant they put it into their mouth, it falls

Chapter 3 The Workings of Human Reincarnation

apart and can't be eaten. They grow thinner and thinner, and their bellies swell with hunger. Those whose sins are particularly profound are strung naked and upside-down in this hell.

There may be many smokers among my readers. You must all be thinking, "If just smoking is such a sin, what kinds of sins will I find when I look back on my life!" For anyone who thinks that, it's never too late. Try starting today to look back and reflect upon what you have done. There is still room for leniency, if we repent our sins in the course of our life and within the 49-day period after death.

Hell is far more severe than any prison. In the material world, for example, if you receive a five-year sentence, once you serve out the term, you are released. Further, in a prison, you would be made to live under strict rules and be forced to do a certain type of work, but you won't be given any suffering that is too hard. But in hell, there is no such thing as a sentence. Unless those cast into hell truly repent from the very bottom of their hearts, they will never be released. This is why the periods of atonement can easily take hundreds of years.

To make things worse, in hell, you must also reflect and repent your actions in the midst of pain and suffering given, such as the freezing cold of the Frozen Hell, and the hunger of the Realm of Hungry Ghosts. The deceased, now using their astral bodies, are not allowed to die, though. No matter how bad the suffering, they must bear it and atone for their sins. Hearing this, there may be many who think that hell is scary or that deities who would cast us into hell are too harsh. But when we complete 30 lives of practice, any one of us can ascend to the Realm of Deity (in five-dimensional space).[23] We must go through this harsh punishment for our sins and repent of them sincerely, precisely because we can someday become gods.

As we come to understand the errors of our ways and our own shortcomings in the midst of all this horrible suffering, we can rise up to higher levels of the Astral Realm. And eventually, at some point, you will be able to get out of hell altogether. Once you're out of hell, there are other places for atonement above that, namely, levels for heavy labor, light labor, a place where you at least can read books, and a place where you can cultivate yourself to some levels. In the level for heavy labor, for example, you will be worked to the bone from morning to night, doing heavy, repetitive labor (e.g., carrying stones, dirt, or sand). There is no suffering such as there is in the hells here, but we atone for our sins by performing this labor over and over without an ounce of joy.

As you come to realize your own errors, you will rise up

Chapter 3 The Workings of Human Reincarnation

through these levels. When deities judge that you have truly repented your sins from your life, and that you have completely eliminated all attachment to the Present Realm, you have completed the final step in which some level of self-cultivation is possible, and will finally be allowed to end your atonement in the Astral Realm. At that time, you will be able to return to everyone who has been waiting for you in your true home in the Spirit Realm.

---

[21] Accurately speaking, suicides are not sent to the Frozen Hell as soon as they are divinely judged on the 49th day after death. Suicides become earthbound spirits, and are tied to the actual location in the Present Realm in which they committed suicide. Even while they are in that place, as soon as they die they are made to experience the same state as if they were in the Frozen Hell (for more details, see Section 3-9).

[22] This is merely an example of one of the laws of the universe (divine rule). The law of the universe (divine role) clearly defines what kinds of words, deeds, personalities, and ideas are considered to be sins, and can cause people to be cast into predetermined hell. However, there are not enough pages in this book to explain it completely.

[23] More accurately, this doesn't necessarily mean that just anyone can complete 30 lives of practice. When souls and spirit bodies are created in the Spirit Realm, 10 lives of practice are given unconditionally. But if they still show no signs of improvement even after they have experienced 10 lives, their souls and spirit bodies are eliminated by deities.

From the graveyard of the Astral Realm to the Spirit Realm

A deceased person who is to return to the Spirit Realm will

be taken by the one watcher spirit who has been accompanying them to date up to the highest level of the Astral Realm, where their grave is. They are inside a large building. In your grave, you will find all of the astral bodies you have used in your lives of practice up to that point, lined up from the newest in the very front to the oldest as they were when you died in your lives.[24] For example, you may see that your astral body in the very front was that of a Japanese samurai, and the second one was that of an Arab woman, and so on. They are all different and all in order.

As you look at each of the bodies in order from the most recent to the oldest, all of the memories erased before will come back all at once. Your memories, for example, of childhoods in previous lives, your life as a samurai, the hell you fell to after you died, and your subsequent return to the Spirit Realm, will all come back to you as soon as you see your astral bodies lined up there.

You will look back over your entire past up to that point, finally coming back to the memory of when your soul was first created in the Spirit Realm. After all of these memories have come back to you, now you shed your current astral body, and place it in the front position in the graveyard. (This is the death of the astral body.) In this way, the deceased returns to their spirit body, which has the youth of a 20-year-old.

The deceased, having returned to their original form, puts on their own clothes, and is led to the entrance of the Spirit Realm by their watcher spirit.[25] There is a wall at the border between the Spirit Realm and the Astral Realm, and in that wall there is a gate which serves as the entrance to the Spirit Realm. This gate is roughly 3 meters (about 10 feet) wide, and is outfitted with a sturdy door equipped with hardware and roof. The gate is watched over by guards, inhabitants of the Spirit Realm, who open the door when a watcher spirit brings back the deceased. As the deceased goes through that gate, they enter again into the Spirit Realm.

When you go through the gate, all of your true family and relatives who live in the Spirit Realm will be there for an emotional reunion. At this point, the one watcher spirit who has stayed with you for so long will hand you over to your family, and then depart. Having finished your long odyssey, you are finally back in the Spirit Realm!

The spirits of the deceased, upon returning to the Spirit Realm, attend lectures by gods in seven-dimensional space for five hours a day for the first week after their return. These lectures are orientation sessions, and their content is concerned with the laws and workings of the Spirit Realm, and with the work each spirit does there. Because a very long time has passed while the spirit of the deceased was engaged in practice in the Present Realm and atonement in the Astral Realm, there are sometimes changes in the Spirit Realm in all that time. This is why the spirits of the deceased all take part in these orientation sessions. When the orientation is over, you can continue to live freely in the Spirit Realm under the guidance of deities until it is time for your next incarnation in the Present Realm.

This is the truth about the world before we are born as humans, the significance of our births in this life, and the worlds we go to after our deaths. This is the system in which we live. Hopefully this true knowledge of the workings of the universe will provide you with insight on how you should live from now on.

[24] As astral bodies do not decompose, even astral bodies used eons ago are preserved. No astral bodies remain from transmigrated lives spent as animals, however.

[25] The watcher spirit brings these clothes in advance from the Spirit Realm in accordance with the wishes of the deceased.

3-8 The issues of organ donation and transplants

Though I touched upon it briefly in Section 3-5, I would

● Revised Organ Transplant Law in Japan (Revised July 2009, effective July 2010)

	Prior to revision	After revision
Age	15 years and over	No age restriction (Excludes children who have lived less than 12 weeks after birth.)
Conditions	In addition to the consent of the family, the will of the donor to donate must be documented (by a donor card).	As long as the family's consent is obtained, the will of the patient does not need to be addressed (no donor card is necessary).
The position on brain death	Considered the death of the person when the will to donate has been expressed.	Brain death is equivalent to actual death of the person.

like to discuss the problems involved with organ donation, which has attracted some attention recently.

The Organ Transplant Law in Japan was revised in July of 2009 to define brain death as the "death of a person," and also to do away with age restrictions on organ donation.

Let's take a moment here to explain exactly what sort of state "brain death" is in the first place. Put simply, brain death refers to the cessation of the functions of the entire brain (the cerebrum, cerebellum, brainstem, and so on) with no foreseeable recovery. What is important here is that the functions of the brainstem are also stopped. The brainstem controls the

● **An overview of the brain**

Cerebrum

Cerebellum

Brainstem

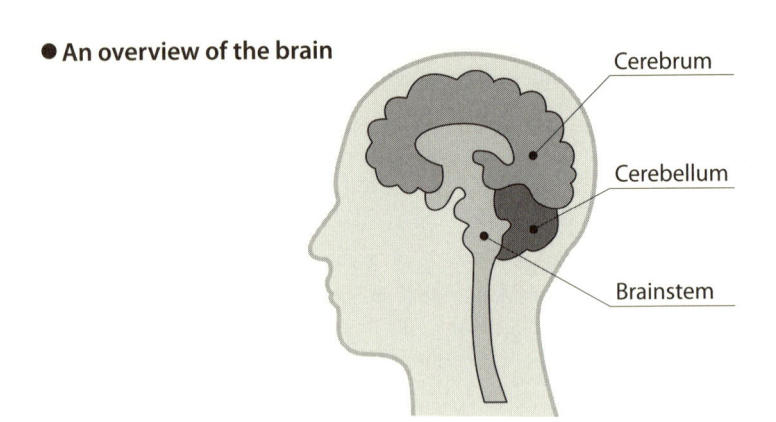

most important functions that a person needs to stay alive, including respiration and the very beating of our hearts. For this reason, when the functions of the brainstem are stopped in brain death, unless some means of artificial respiration is used, respiration stops right away, leading to cardiac death.

On the other hand, however, even when the brainstem stops functioning, by utilizing artificial respiration, the heart and the other organs can function normally, and the individual is able to live for a long time in a state of sleep. These individuals, apart from the functioning of their brain, are completely alive, and they have warm blood being pumped through their veins. They sweat, produce waste, and their hair and nails continue to grow.

For example, to cite a newspaper report from May of 2009,

Chapter 3 The Workings of Human Reincarnation

the reporter spoke with the 50-year-old son who had been caring for his mother, who was brain-dead. This is what he told the reporter: "What I have been surprised by after spending day and night by her side is that, when I shed tears thinking of the parting that is to come, my mother also sheds tears along with me." Another report in June 2009 introduced the parents of a small girl, just a year and seven months old, who was sleeping in brain death. They said to the reporters: "Her expression is always peaceful, just like she's sleeping. We can see the changes in her expression from day to day." So do you think that it's OK to excise the organs of people in this state?

I have been taught clearly by God that:

"Even those who are 'brain-dead' are still alive."

Because there is no way for those experiencing brain death to express their wishes by speaking or gesturing, there are many, including doctors and nurses, who consider these people to have no consciousness, and be equivalent to dead. But in actual fact, brain-dead patients are still alive, and they retain consciousness.

Brain death is the same as sleep paralysis
There may be some among my readers who have experi-

enced sleep paralysis before. Sleep paralysis refers to a state of being completely conscious, but unable to move one's body at all, in other words, being able to hear, but unable to move the hands or feet, open the eyes, or speak, which primarily occurs when falling asleep.

You can think of being in sleep paralysis as an easy way to understand what brain death is like. That is to say, your soul and spirit body are completely conscious, but you are unable to use your body. When we think about it this way, a brain-dead patient having their organs extracted is just the same as having their organs ripped out and taken from them while they are in sleep paralysis.

Of course, the patient can hear the conversations of the doctors and nurses, and they know that their organs will be donated. No matter how they scream "No! Stop! Don't take my organs!" inside themselves, there is absolutely nothing that they can do. Then, the intense pain of the organs being ripped from the body of the patient is carried over into the astral body that the patient will use when they die. We have to understand that this is what "brain-dead" individuals who have their organs removed for donation go through.

Also, as explained in Section 3-5, even in the case of cardiac death rather than brain death, the astral body is still directly connected with a spirit cord to the physical body (the remains) after death. So this cannot accurately be called "true death." This is why the pain and suffering of those whose remains are harmed by autopsies and organ donation after cardiac death is carried over into their astral bodies. The face of the deceased screws up in agony as they watch their remains being harmed from just about 60 centimeters (about 2 feet) above.

I will say this again: it's not over when we die. After we die, a period of atonement in the Astral Realm awaits us, which could last decades, or even hundreds of years. The pain and suffering inflicted upon the physical body will remain present throughout the duration of this atonement.

The same rule applies to eye donation as well as other organ donation like hearts and kidneys. Eye donors will have to spend a long, difficult period of atonement in the Astral Realm as a blind person.

3-9 On suicide: the importance of living every moment

At the present time, more than 1 million people worldwide end their own lives every year, and the number is over 30,000 every year in Japan alone. If we do the math, that comes out to nearly 100 Japanese committing suicide every day. In fact, it's said that the number of attempted suicides is 10 times of the number of actual suicides.

There are all sorts of reasons that people commit suicide. It could be worries about health, financial problems, family problems, troubles at work, troubles in love, bullying at school, and on and on. Most of those who commit suicide probably feel that, if they are able to escape from their current reality, they can die and go to nothingness, or that if they die it will get easier. But the point that I want to consistently drive home to you in this book is that *it is not over when we die*, and that *dying is not necessarily going to make anything easier*. This is why you must absolutely never commit suicide.

As I explained in Section 2-3, physical pain just before death remains in the astral body. I'd like to tell you about what a god taught me about what it's like for suicides when they die. He told me that, if there were any way he could, he wants to show this to all of humankind. If he did, then absolutely no one would commit suicide.

The wounds of those who died by cutting their wrists hurt incredibly. The pain experienced by the astral body is many times that felt while alive. That is why suicides crawl on the earth in pain, streaming blood.

Those that died by hanging themselves repeat desperate attempts to claw the rope from around their neck in order to be free.

Those who drowned themselves will roll around and around on the ground in suffering, unable to breathe.

The bodies of those who killed themselves by jumping in front of a train are torn to pieces, meaning their astral body also exists in tragic pieces.

Recently, the number of people who commit suicide using hydrogen sulfide has been increasing. It seems that many people think that this is an easy and painless way to die. But they are totally wrong. Just before people die by hydrogen sulfide, they feel pain in their body as if it were melting. A pain that feels as if you are rotting alive envelops your entire body.

And, as I explained in Section 3-7, deities regard suicide as the greatest sin, no matter what the reason is. This is why when suicides die, their painful condition is preserved in the Frozen Hell, to experience even further suffering as they petrify in the freezing cold.

And yet there is still more suffering in store for the suicide. Those who died unnatural deaths (people who died by suicide, murder, or some accident) are tethered by deities to the spot where they died. If they are barely able to move, it is only within about 50 meters (about 55 yards) in radius. These are called earthbound spirits. An earthbound spirit doesn't have anything to do with their vigil, funeral, or divine judgment held on the 49th day after death. Earthbound spirits are essentially bound to that spot forever, unable to move on.[26] That is why famous battlegrounds of long ago in Japan and around the world still have so many earthbound spirits, suffering invisibly there for centuries.

There are also situations in which traffic accidents and other incidents occur repeatedly in the same spot. This happens because the earthbound spirit left by the first accident is lonely and in pain, and ends up pulling others in. These earthbound spirits are made to exist in hell in the same condition directly after their death, without receiving divine judgment. The type of hell depends on the sins a person has committed. For suicides, it is the Frozen Hell described earlier.

In this way, rather than becoming nothing or feeling better when we commit suicide, we will be dealt a trifecta of suffering—our suffering that is carried over into our astral body, our suffering in the Frozen Hell, and the suffering involved with being an earthbound spirit. Suicides lament this trifecta of suffering, and greatly regret having taken their own life.

But human life is filled with a great deal of worries and pain. We may feel at times that we want to kill ourselves when we are faced head-on with these worries and pain. So how should we continue to live at these times?

In times like that, try to think about why you have to worry and why you have to suffer. It will fall into one of the categories below.

[26] In the course of my travels around Japan to give lectures, I am often asked whether loved ones who died unnatural deaths can be saved. In fact, there are ways to save earthbound spirits. However, because these can vary from person to person, this isn't a question that can be fully answered in this book.

Reflecting on your life up to now

When you trace your suffering back to its origin, you will often find that it is caused by your own actions or traits. That is to say, the life that you have led up to now is reflected in your current life.

For example, let's say that you are in trouble with debt. But isn't that, after all, caused by your own reckless nature and habits of frivolous spending? Of course there's nothing you can do about debt you already have, but the important thing is to correct these traits and habits. If you have a tendency to be depressed and blame yourself for everything, things will only get worse. If you try instead to accept yourself as you are, and try to always live facing forward, your worries and your suffering will be relieved before you know it.

Trials given to us by deities

As I keep repeating in this book, the Present Realm is a place to practice and cultivate our souls. There are times when God and other deities give you further worries and suffering as trials in order to cultivate your soul. That is why a long, full life will have more trouble and suffering times than easy or fun times. God and other deities watch over you tenderly, hoping that you will be able to rise to the challenge, and allow your soul to grow, completing your practice in the Present Realm.

Reflecting on your past lives

All of the lives you have led as practice already in the Present Realm are by no means separate. This life, your previous life, the one before that, and all of your lives to come, are all connected. The conditions of your current life have a lot to do with how you lived your former lives. For example, if you caused the suffering of others in a previous life, as a result, you will be given the same suffering by God and other deities in your current life. This is how our past lives are reflected on our current incarnations.

I'm often told, when I talk about past lives, that they don't matter because we have no memory of them. There are many who wonder what they should do. They're completely right. Just as how you lived your past lives has so much to do with your current life, how you live this life will greatly influence your future lives.

Even if, for example, you are surrounded by unhappy circumstances, and you don't seem to have been blessed with much, live fervently in devotion to others. If you do, God and other deities will surely guide you to happiness in the next life. The important thing is to keep persevering and living for the moment, accepting troubles and suffering as they come. This will lead you to happiness in future lives. Please don't ever forget this fact.

This chapter has covered the workings of human rebirth in some detail. I'm sure that many of my readers are surprised at the grand scale of this system. Every day we face an array of troubles and suffering. We suffer from disease, hardships of life, anxieties about the future, and troubles at home, in love, at the workplace, at school, and so on.

But if you take all of these troubles and suffering and put them in the context of the grand scheme of things, aren't they just the most pathetic little things? This is nothing more than one mere instant of pain or suffering, out of only one of the many lives you have experienced since your soul was created in the Spirit Realm so long ago. By cultivating our souls through overcoming these obstacles, we complete our life practice. And when we experience 30 lives, we can ascend to the Realm of Deity as a god.

"Humankind is given life by God and other deities in this grand system."

I want all of my readers to live in awareness of the larger system on a daily basis for the rest of your lives. If you do, I know that something will change. You will come to be able to let the petty troubles go, and lead a bright and vibrant life. You may even come to repent of the way you have been living, and your life may even take a turn for the better because of that. My hope is that as many people as possible will read this book, and change their lives.

Chapter 4

The Future of Earth and Humanity

4-1 The state of Earth

In recent years, many have taken notice of how strange the climate has been, and how the occurrence of natural disasters has grown.

Climate change

In 2009, the rainy season in Japan ended much later than expected. Especially in Hokuriku and Tohoku regions, where the rainy season normally ends with July, there were still many rainy days, the wet and cloudy weather continuing until the middle of August, and no definite end to the rainy season was established. Again in summer 2010, the Japanese islands have been threatened by record heat. Even in late summer, an extraordinary level of heat continued, and autumn couldn't come soon enough. The changing of the seasons has become blurred.

Abnormal meteorological phenomena have been occurring all over the globe recently. We are seeing extreme phenomena such as heat waves in some areas and cold waves in others all over Earth. Record heat waves hit Europe in the summer of 2003, for example. The dead in France and Germany numbered over 50,000, being mostly the elderly who lived in buildings without air conditioning. But from January to February of

2008, China suffered a serious cold wave. High-voltage transmission lines were down by avalanches, and power was out, affecting people's lifelines. Over 100 people died as a result, and the afflicted people are said to number over 100 million.

Heat waves and cold waves occurred in 2010, too. Threatened by a heat wave, western Russia and Siberia have seen the highest temperatures ever in 130 years of recorded history. For some time, the daily temperature average was 9 to 10 degrees Celsius (about 16 to 18 degrees Fahrenheit) above the historical average. Because of the heat, the number of Russians who drowned by trying to deal with the heat with water is over 2,000, which is abnormal. The other side of the globe, which was heading into winter at the same time, was visited by record cold. In Bolivia in South America, snow fell in regions where there had never been recorded snowfall. Snowdrifts caused power outages and obstructed traffic in Chile, isolating towns. There were reports that in western Brazil 27,000 head of livestock were lost due to the cold temperatures.

Heat waves and cold waves alone are not abnormal weather. On this Earth, there are places that are drying out and undergoing desertification, and there are other places where downpour occurs. Especially in the last few years, we've grown used to the term *guerilla downpour* being used in Japan to describe sudden, torrential rains. These localized rains have caused flooding of lowlands and rivers, as well as mudslides all over the country. These floods and mudslides are occurring not only in Japan, but all over the world. In mid-June of 2010, in China, for example, record-breaking torrential downpours continued, causing huge flooding. The floodwaters flowed into the towns, destroying buildings and causing severe damage.

It's not just these guerilla downpours that cause floods and landslides. In the last few years, tropical storms like typhoons have been growing in size, and causing a huge amount of damage all around the world. In late August of 2005, for example, the southeastern United States was hit by the super hurricane Katrina. Katrina broke through the reservoirs and levees of the Mississippi River, and 80 percent of the entire land area of the city of New Orleans, Louisiana, was under water. Then, people began to see the tragic sight of the dead, their bodies floating on the surface of the water. In August of 2009, Typhoon Morakot hit Taiwan, causing enormous floods including landslides and flooding. Over 600 people were reported dead or missing. According to the local media, it was the "worst typhoon damage in southern Taiwan in the past 50 years."

The continuation of big earthquakes

In the last few years, big earthquakes have occurred over

Chapter 4 The Future of Earth and Humanity

and over in Japan. For example, in 2007, earthquakes measuring 5.0 or greater on the JMA Seismic Intensity Scale occurred eight times (the Noto Peninsula Earthquake, the Niigata Chuetsu Earthquake, etc.), and six occurred in 2008 (the Iwate-Miyagi Inland Earthquake, etc.).

To turn our eyes abroad, giant earthquakes such as those that used to only occur every few decades are now occurring continually in recent years. On December 26, 2004, in Aceh Province of Sumatra Island in Indonesia, an earthquake with a magnitude estimated to be between 9.1 and 9.3 occurred (the Sumatra Earthquake). It's said that this is the second largest magnitude for an earthquake since 1900. The tsunami that was generated by this earthquake (the Asian Tsunami) reached Indonesia, Thailand, Malaysia, India, Sri Lanka, the Maldives, and even to Africa, bringing unprecedented losses of life, with a total of over 2 million afflicted, and roughly 230,000 dead or missing. This number from the combined earthquake and tsunami is said to be the third highest for a natural disaster on the face of Earth since the year 1900.

An earthquake occurred in 2008 in China's Sichuan Province, where over 80,000 people lost their lives. Huge earthquakes continued to occur frequently in 2010 as well. In January, the number of dead from the Haiti Earthquake rose

- Cracks in the earth made by the Sumatra Earthquake (in interior Aceh)

- The graves on the third day after the disaster
  (For weeks after the tsunami, no matter how many bodies were moved, there were more left all over the town, letting off a noxious smell.)

Chapter 4 The Future of Earth and Humanity

above 200,000, rivaling the death toll from the Sumatra Earthquake. Then in February, the Chile Earthquake estimated to have a magnitude of 8.8 occurred. In April, an enormous earthquake happened in Qinghai Province, China, and many people lost their lives. The earthquakes continued throughout 2011. Many Japanese students studying in New Zealand's South Island were lost to the magnitude 6.1 earthquake that occurred there in Christchurch in February. Then, on March 11th, the earthquake off the Pacific coast of the Tohoku region struck with a magnitude of 9.0, the largest in Japan in recorded history. The number of those dead or missing as a result of this earthquake, followed by tsunami waves and aftershocks (the Great East Japan Earthquake), has climbed to roughly 20,000.

Huge eruptions

In the spring of 2010, Iceland's glacier-capped volcano Eyjafjallajökull erupted for the first time since 1823. At the time, the caldera of the volcano was covered with ice nearly 300 meters (about 1,000 feet) thick. The water from the melting ice contacted with magma creating steam, and triggered the phreatomagmatic eruption. The melting of the glacier also became the source of large-scale flooding. Due to the effects of large amounts of volcanic ash, all air traffic in northwestern Europe was thrown into a state of confusion. Similarly, in August of 2010, on the northern part of the Indonesian island

● Major large-scale disasters in 2010 and 2011

Month	Summary of the disaster
January 2010	A cold wave hits northern China, bringing huge snows (with temperatures -16°C [3.2°F] recorded in Beijing)
	Galeras in Colombia in South America erupts, leaving over 8,000 homeless
	M 7.0 earthquake occurs in Haiti, roughly 200,000 perished (Haiti Earthquake)
	Tremendous cold waves hit all of Europe, many die (with temperatures -35°C [-31°F] recorded in Eastern Europe)
February 2010	The worst heat wave in 50 years hits Rio de Janeiro, Brazil (with temperatures up to 46.3°C [115.3°F] recorded and sensible temperatures above 50°C [122°F], many elderly people perished)
	M 8.8 earthquake in Chile (Chile Earthquake)
March 2010	Landslides occurring due to guerilla downpours in eastern Uganda (multiple villages were buried, leaving over 80 dead and around 400 missing)
	M 6.4 earthquake in southern Taiwan (largest in the Kaohsiung district for the past 100 years)
	Worst drought in 100 years in southwest China (over 20 million people faced drinking water shortages)
	A volcano near Iceland's Eyjafjallajökull glacier erupts for the first time since 1823 (there were also subsequent eruptions in April and May, causing flooding due to the melting of the glacier)
April 2010	M 7.1 earthquake in Qinghai, China, over 2000 dead
	Large numbers of deaths in various parts of India due to unseasonal heat waves (with temperatures 43.7°C [110.7°F] recorded in New Delhi)
June 2010	Hurricane Alex hits land in Mexico's northeastern state of Tamaulipas (nearly all 250,000 residents of the capital, Ciudad Victoria, had no power or water)
July 2010	Cold waves all across South America (-14°C [6.8°F] recorded in Argentina, and even in tropical Bolivia, where normally the temperature is never below 20°C [68°F], temperatures dropped to near 0°C [32°F])
	Record-breaking heat in Russia (highest temperature in recorded history in Moscow, forest fires and drownings occurred in succession)
	Heavy rains and flooding over a wide area of China (flooding and landslides in the Yangtze River basin caused many deaths, 30,000 left helpless due to flooding in Jilin Province)
	Large scale flooding in northwestern Pakistan for the first time in 80 years (Pakistan Flood)
August 2010	Heavy rains continue further in China (over 1,200 dead by debris avalanches in Gansu Province in the northwest of China, and roughly 250,000 were displaced by flooding of the Yalu River in Liaoning Province at the border of North Korea)
	Casualties from the flooding in the Pakistan Flood continue to grow (over 3,800 dead and 17 million injured)
	Mount Sinabung on northern Sumatra Island in Indonesia erupts for the first time in about 400 years

Chapter 4 The Future of Earth and Humanity

October 2010	M 7.7 earthquake off the coast of Sumatra Island in Indonesia (with aftershocks of M 6.1), producing a huge tsunami (over 500 dead or missing)
	Mount Merapi on central Java in Indonesia erupts, tens of thousands left homeless
	Heaviest downpours in recorded history on Amami-Oshima Island in Kagoshima Prefecture, Japan
December 2010	Unprecedented cold waves in Europe, airports closed
	M 6.5 earthquake in southeastern Iran (buildings collapsed, many buried alive)
January 2011	The worst cold wave in 40 years hit New Delhi, India, causing numerous deaths
	Sri Lanka suffers extensive damage from torrential rains, over one million people are affected
	Mount Shinmoe, on the border between Kagoshima and Miyazaki Prefectures, erupts
February 2011	Enormous Cyclone Yasi makes landfall in Australia
	M 6.1 earthquake hits Christchurch, in southern New Zealand (NZ Earthquake)
March 2011	The Great East Japan Earthquake (M 9.0 earthquake off the Pacific coast of the Tohoku region, followed by tsunami waves and aftershocks)
April 2011	More than 300 people die from severe storms and tornadoes that strike the southern United States (Alabama, etc.)
May 2011	Tornadoes occur in Missouri, in the United States (over 100 people died)
June 2011	The Puyehue volcano, in southern Chile, erupts for the first time in half a century
	Torrential rains continue for over a week in inland China (over 100 died, more than 55,000 fled for safety)
July 2011	Mount Lokon, in Indonesia, has a major eruption (volcanic ash and molten lava were blasted 1500 meters up into the air)
	Heat wave in central Russia (in Volgograd, the temperature exceeded 40°C [104°F] for 3 consecutive days)
August 2011	In Baghdad and southern Iraq, the temperature exceeds 50°C [122°F]
	Centered in Virginia, M 5.8 earthquake hits the eastern United States, the biggest earthquake in decades to strike the East Coast
	Over 40 people die in the United States and Canada as a result of Hurricane Irene
September 2011	Enormous damage, centered in Nara and Wakayama, Japan is caused by Typhoon No. 12 (over 50 people died due to the flooding of rivers, mudslides, etc)
October 2011	Record-setting flood damage occurs in Thailand (about one-third of the country was submerged)
	M 7.2 earthquake hits southeast Turkey, causing numerous deaths

Note: This list has been compiled based on the latest information from various media sources (newspapers, the Internet, etc.), but reports of the scale of disasters and the number of missing and dead may change with the passage of time.

113

of Sumatra, the Mount Sinabung, which had been classified as dormant for a long time, erupted for the first time in roughly 400 years. Tens of thousands of people living in the area were displaced and left nowhere to go. Then, in February of 2011, Shinmoedake, a volcano situated on the border between Kagoshima and Miyazaki Prefectures, Japan, erupted.

Those are just a few of the natural disasters that have occurred in recent years. You may find yourself surprised at the number of large-scale disasters occurring even only in recent times. You may also be surprised to find that a particularly high number of natural disasters have happened since the year 2010. I have put together a list of all the main large-scale disasters that have happened since the year 2010.

The natural disasters I've included in my list here are only a small portion of the disasters that have actually happened on Earth from 2010. Even for only a partial list, this is a great lot of disaster. Earth is crying out in anguish and causing natural disasters one after another, as if angered by the absurd destruction of the environment that humankind is perpetrating.

The occurrence of various infectious diseases

Humanity has experienced many viral epidemics, including Ebola, dengue fever, AIDS, SARS, and on and on. In recent

Chapter 4 The Future of Earth and Humanity

years, we've also had a new strain of the flu (H1N1) and foot-and-mouth disease, and the infectious outbreaks have even hit close to home for Japanese. Aside from viral epidemics, we are also being warned of other epidemics caused by new strains of bacteria against which antibiotics are ineffective (also known as super-resistant bacteria). I will explain in further detail about various diseases again in Section 4-5.

4-2 Towards the evolution of Earth and humankind

The continuing occurrence of these climatic fluctuations and natural disasters, along with the appearance of a variety of infectious diseases, suggests that our current civilization, just like that of the end days of the Mu civilization, is in its final phase. Right now, God and other deities are preparing to cleanse Earth and humanity again for the second time.

From here on out, even more people will lose their lives due to these continuing large-scale natural disasters and sundry diseases, and the curtain will close on the civilization of this Earth. Most people, when they hear this, either can't or don't want to believe it. It's natural for us, as humans, to feel as though we don't want to believe things that are so odious to us, or that we want to forget them. But I will say it again and again throughout this book. Civilization on this Earth will actually come to an end.

This is not necessarily a bad thing, however. God and other deities are right now trying to allow Earth and humanity to evolve to the next step by a complete cleansing. The extinction of our current civilization is the unavoidable pain of birth that must be endured in order to better Earth and humankind.

Right now, Earth is crying out in pain. We humans have finally pushed it beyond its breaking point with excessive destruction of forests and extraction of fossil fuels, as well as the gases and waste water produced by factories that causes pollution in the air, water, and land. I'm sure you remember the crude-oil spill that happened in the Gulf of Mexico in the spring of 2010. This incident caused as much as 9.8 million liters (about 2.6 million US gallons,/,2.2 million UK gallons) of crude oil to flow into the Gulf of Mexico, causing enormous damage to the ecosystem there.[27] In the wetlands on the land nearest the oil well where the spill occurred, in Louisiana, all sorts of wildlife, including pelicans, seals, gulls, and so on, were found to be covered in the oil from the spill.

A god has compared this spill to a person having an artery cut, thus bleeding unstoppably. On this analogy, the spill would be a serious injury for Earth. Just by watching the news

Chapter 4 The Future of Earth and Humanity

reports of this incident on television and reading in the papers, it is easy to see that the destruction of Earth's environment and ecosystems are already at a stage too advanced for us to do anything about. This planet, which has been ruined by the hands of humanity, will be restored and made new by the hands of God and other deities. In this new world that they will create, the beauty of nature that once was will be restored.

Earth is not the only thing that will be created anew, however. Human civilization will also be made new.

As I explained at the end of the first chapter, the biggest reason why the hearts of people in this day and age have gone astray is that they have forgotten the existence of deities, believing too much in their own abilities, and that they have mistakenly come to believe that the present, visible world is all that there is. In order to warn and admonish those who believe this, God and other deities will continue to make these large-scale natural disasters and epidemics occur. Through this process, only those with pure hearts, who believe in deities, will be chosen to be saved. Those who survive will go on to someday build a new civilization on new Earth.

The civilization to come will not be a materially-based civilization like the present one. It will be more properly, a spiritually-based civilization. As those left there will believe in the existence of deities and of worlds invisible, they won't sin. Of course, the selfish mindset that allows us to do anything as long as it is good for us, and as long as we can profit, will never sully the face of this Earth again. For that reason, this new world will be as wonderful as heaven. In that sense, the coming extinction of our current civilization will be the first step towards a brilliant and glorious future.

So in concrete terms, what will be involved in the progress towards the end of the current civilization?

God has revealed these things to me in some detail:

What will happen with global warming?
Where and how will huge earthquakes and eruptions occur?
What about economic and social conditions from here on out?
What about the movements of diseases like the new strain of influenza?
And more.

In the next section, I will introduce a very small portion of the answers to all of these questions.[28] Still, please consider the information I will reveal below to be the divine plan as of the spring of 2012. God and other deities are monitoring us in real time. The conditions they are considering include things as divergent as the political and social conditions of countries throughout this world, and the content of the heart of each and every person living on Earth. They will determine how things play out in the end days of our civilization based on a precise understanding of all of these conditions. That is why at the current stage, there is a good possibility that the plan will be changed to some extent as we move forward.

Think about the conditions of humanity on this Earth right now. There is no end to the civil wars, terrorism, and other conflict happening. Even on the individual level, there is a large number of people who believe in their selfish hearts. They don't matter what they do to other people as long as it's good for themselves, or if it can at least make them money. This is the current state of humanity.

If a certain level of improvement in the human condition is seen, God will change his plan to delay the end of our civilization somewhat. The later the final days arrive, the more people in the world will come to realize the errors of their ways, and will begin to repent. The more people like that increase, the more people will survive the extinction of this civilization. As I pointed out in Chapter 2, that is exactly the goal of this book.

[27] According to reports on July 15, 2010, it became clear that the British company BP, which was doing the work in the oil fields where the spill occurred, was able to install a "cap" on the places leaking crude oil, and that the outflow had nearly been stopped. Then in September, they succeeded in sealing the well completely.

[28] In our lectures, now held all over Japan, we provide updates on changes to the plane of God in real time. Please consider attending one of our lectures if you would like to get the latest information.

4-3 Our environment: climate change and natural disasters

Global warming and climate change

According to the divine plan, after a time the pace of global warming will be much quicker than has been estimated by scientists. From here on out, as global warming progresses, it will bring even more intense climate changes on a global scale.

Strong winds will blow every day, sometimes violent, damaging gales. The ice at the South Pole will melt, and, when the sea level rises, these gusting winds will also cause tsunamis. This will be an age of crazy weather. Because changes in the weather will become more sudden and violent, the weather will be even more difficult to predict. These gusty winds will also cause subsequent problems with airplane crashes. When this happens, people will no doubt begin to get nervous. No matter how much we talk about measures to stop global warming, like

Chapter 4 The Future of Earth and Humanity

using natural energies, it is already too late for any human power to stop it. God has revealed to me that this is what it will be like in the future.

Even in Japan, abnormal weather patterns will become more marked. Sudden thunder and guerilla downpours will occur with greater frequency than ever, and floods and landslides also will continue to increase. Large tornadoes, the likes of which have almost never been seen before in Japan, will occur, hurt people, and damage homes and vehicles.[29]

The distinctions between the seasons will become completely blurred. Someday, despite the fact that it is the middle of summer, it could suddenly start snowing or hailing. We will enter an age where even in summer we won't be able to put away our coats and heaters. The differences in temperature between one day and the next will get more severe. It could be incredibly hot one day, and incredibly cold the next. The differences between daytime and nighttime temperatures will also grow more intense. There will be many who will suffer ill health due to this, their bodies being unable to keep up with the changes in temperature.

---

[29] This is what a god told me on July 1, 2009. Immediately thereafter, the predictions (the divine plans) came true. Then, on the night of July 19, gust-

ing winds thought to be caused by a tornado occurred in the south of Mimasaka in Okayama Prefecture, Japan, damaging some homes and destroying others completely. It also caused other damage including throwing cars over 100 meters (about 110 yards). After that, on the 27th of the same month, there were reports on gusting winds thought to be caused by a tornado. In addition to injuring at least 21 people, it caused damage to vehicles and homes in Tatebayashi, Gunma Prefecture, Japan.

Huge earthquakes and eruptions

Next, God has also planned to bring about a series of gigantic earthquakes and eruptions throughout the world. The fact is that there have been a rash of earthquakes in all parts of Japan since the Great East Japan Earthquake. Going forward, this trend will become even more pronounced.

For example, the Tokai Earthquake is supposed to happen in Suruga Bay in Shizuoka Prefecture, Japan. It is generally predicted that it will be a magnitude 8. The plan of God, though, is for it to be a magnitude 9, and cause an enormous amount of damage. If the motion of that earthquake sets off the Tonankai Earthquake (between the Chukyo and Nanki regions, Japan) and the Nankai Earthquake (between the Nanki and Shikoku regions, Japan), even greater damage is expected.

There will also be an earthquake directly under the capital. In the original plan of God, an earthquake between magnitude

Chapter 4 The Future of Earth and Humanity

7.2 and 7.4 in Japan's Kanto region, where Tokyo lies, was supposed to happen by the year 2012. But I have recently been told that this plan has been delayed. This is because apparently, there has been a marked change in the hearts of the people living in Tokyo and its environs. As a god told me, not all, but many of the people there have begun to realize what "the most important thing of all for humanity" is. That is to say, they are coming to wake up to the fact that, rather than chasing after money and material possessions, they should be loving and caring for others. Thanks to this, God has made the decision to delay the occurrence of these earthquakes directly beneath metropolitan areas to see how humanity will do for a little while longer.

On top of that, a large scale eruption of Mount Fuji, Japan, will also occur. Fuji's eruption is planned to be set off by the earthquakes mentioned above. A god has said that the insects and other animals will begin to behave abnormally prior to the eruption (see the column "Insects and animals predicting the future?!").

These gigantic earthquakes, eruptions, and other natural disasters are not merely physical phenomena. These phenomena have the purpose of providing a chance for humanity, which has forgotten deities and grown overly self-satisfied, to understand their own powerlessness, and to recognize and repent the errors of their ways. They are warnings from God and other deities to reprimand humanity, which has grown wicked. That is why these warnings can be delayed if we only change our hearts for the better.

Still, this doesn't mean that God has canceled his plan for earthquakes directly under cities. In fact, he has been very clear that these earthquakes and the eruption of Mount Fuji will certainly happen in the near future. Right now, however, God and other deities are intently monitoring us humans in order to decide exactly when to make those happen.

Column: Insects and animals predicting the future?!

It is often said in Japan that there will be a lot of snow in years where there are a lot of stink bugs. Indeed, it often does end up that way. But why is this?

A god spoke to me of the veracity of this.

I was taught that, because the hearts and souls of insects and animals are pure, they still have the ability of prescience. When humankind was placed on this Earth, we also had this same ability. As knowledge and civilization advanced, however, our souls became clouded, and our ability of prescience atrophied.

"Bees build their nests low to the ground in years when there will be big typhoons."
"Every single mouse will leave a house before there is a fire."
"The birds and animals move just before great earthquakes and shifting of Earth."

All of these sayings, which are common folk wisdom in Japan, point to the prescient abilities of animals and insects. This also means that deities uses animals and insects to let us humans, who have lost this ability, know about changes like this. When there are large quantities of stink bugs, this is deities telling us that a lot of snow is coming in the winter, and that we had better start preparing now. From now on, try observing animals and insects in order to be ready for the coming eruption and earthquakes.

4-4 Economic and social conditions

When the large US investment bank Lehman Brothers collapsed in September of 2008, it caused waves of the recession in Japan as well. When governmental power in Japan changed hands from those of the Liberal Democratic Party of Japan to the Democratic Party of Japan in 2009, many people had high hopes for the new administration.

However, their platform floundered, and subsequently they became caught up in "money and politics" and the problems surrounding the relocation of the US air base Futenma in Okinawa. All of the hopes that had been placed on them turned to disillusionment. Now, the nation of Japan has been put it in an even more perilous position. In particular, the nation's finances have completely deteriorated, and currently, the total of the national and regional debts has exceeded 1 quadrillion yen. In a sense, it wouldn't be surprising at all if Japan completely collapsed any time now. Japan is experiencing other problems in addition to the national debt, including negative population growth with an aging population, the hollowing out of domestic industry, pension problems, educational problems, medical problems, and territorial disputes with neighboring countries.

China, on the other hand, made the fastest recovery in the world from the failure of Lehman Brothers, and is now in a period of high-level economic growth (so-called the bubble

Chapter 4 The Future of Earth and Humanity

period). With the Olympic Games held in Beijing in 2008, and the Shanghai World Expo in 2010, they are now in a period of bubble growth similar to that of post-war Japan.

How will these economic and social affairs develop in the future, both in Japan and in the world?

I have been told the following by a god regarding these issues:

China's bubble period will not last long. India will also experience a bubble period, but this will also fall apart. You are already in a worldwide depression. Things that could not have been imagined are going to happen one after another, and the value of currency will drop, and eventually it will have none. Money will become meaningless no matter how much you have. You could try to wipe your nose with it, but it's really too rough for that, so tissues would in fact be of more use. When the effects of global warming bring on worldwide food shortages, it will be comparable to all money losing its value.

In this way, the world's economic and social conditions will continue to deteriorate. Then eventually, we will enter a period of food shortages. Japan is no exception. In fact, as I touched upon in Section 4-1, in the summer of 2009 in Hokuriku and

Tohoku regions, the rainy season did not let up until August, and farmers were vexed by the lack of sunlight. It is thought that climate irregularities caused by global warming will continue. Crops will wither because of these climate irregularities, and food shortages will ensue.

Giant eruptions will also lead to food shortages. To begin with, the high levels of volcanic ash released as an aerosol by the eruption will float up to the stratosphere, there forming a cloud-like layer over a wide area. That layer will act just like an umbrella to stop sunlight. The earth beneath this shade after the eruption will become frigid. This cold will cause crops to whither, which will bring about food shortages.

The eruption of the Laki fissure in Iceland in 1783 is a well-known volcanic disaster from the past. This eruption brought cooling and cold weather damage to the Northern Hemisphere at the time. It is said that, within Iceland, roughly 20 percent of the population perished due to famine. It seems that the effects of this eruption even reached far away Japan. In that year, Mount Asama in Japan also erupted, and it has been pointed out that both of these eruptions contributed to the Great Tenmei Famine in the Tohoku region.

For this reason, there were fears that Iceland's glacier-capped

Chapter 4 The Future of Earth and Humanity

volcano Eyjafjallajökull, which erupted in spring 2010, could bring about the same sort of cooling and cold weather damage. Indeed, I have received this message from a god concerning the volcano in Iceland:

Iceland's volcano has erupted. With this one eruption, all of the products of the civilization you have built will become useless. It will rain volcanic ash, and planes will be unable to fly. Air traffic will be paralyzed. Disappointingly, however, rather than being concerned with what caused such a large-scale eruption, or worrying about whether it could activate other eruptions and earthquakes, you instead seem to be worried only about how much money you will lose due to the financial effects of transportation lines being paralyzed. You humans only want money, which could turn into nothing but paper in the blink of an eye, and you aren't thinking about what will happen when the levels of volcanic ash rise even higher....

The eruptions of the Icelandic volcano will expand further, activating other magma, and if those volcanoes also erupt, the volcanic ash will cover Earth. No matter where you are on the face of Earth, the sun will be hidden, making it dark even in the daytime, and temperatures around the globe will drop suddenly. This, at least, should give humanity a scare.

We must use these giant eruptions as a reason to re-evaluate our way of living, which places emphasis on chasing money and material things.

Column: Tokyo Skytree

Sometimes deities address topics that are closer to home, rather than just those on a global scale. I would like to relate just one of these close-to-home topics to my readers in this book.

Do you know about the Tokyo Skytree?

The Tokyo Skytree is a radio tower, nearly 600 meters (about 2,000 feet) in height, that broadcasts digital television signals since the spring of 2012 by NHK and five commercial broadcasters. It is being called the "new Tokyo Tower." Even during its construction, its height, growing day by day, was already a subject of discussion, and had become a tourist attraction. Before its completion, a god had told me that the Tokyo Skytree would be completed, because the planned earthquakes directly under the city had been delayed until after 2012. Exactly, the Tokyo Skytree has been completed and put into service in the spring of 2012. It is not all roses, however. The god had also told me that, shortly after the completion of the Tokyo Skytree, because of the effects of electromagnetic waves, there will be an increase in people suffering from unexplained ringing in their ears, sudden hearing loss, and even brain tumors. We need to hurry to come up with measures against these electromagnetic waves as soon as possible.

4-5 The movement of infectious diseases

(1) A new strain of influenza

I'm sure that the global outbreak of a new strain of the flu virus (H1N1), which began in Mexico in April of 2009, is still fresh in everyone's memory.[30] When this outbreak of the new flu strain began, serious precautions were taken at airports all over Japan in order to prevent the virus from penetrating the country at its borders. However, the virus slipped through all the precautionary measures, and infiltrated Japan's Kansai region first. In Osaka, Kobe, and other large cities in the region all at the same time, citizens could be seen wearing masks when they went out.

After that, however, the caution that Japanese took when

the outbreak first occurred began to lighten, as if it had never even happened. Why could this be?

The reason is that it became clear that this particular new strain of influenza had a low level of virulence. Simply put, this means that the mortality rate of those infected is low. According to newspaper reports from September 30, 2009, the mortality rate associated with this particular new strain of influenza was no more than 0.045 percent, on the same level as the yearly seasonal strain. This flu strain was originally a low-virulence influenza that spread among swine, and then came to infect humans from swine, and after that, morphed into a virus that can be transmitted from human to human.

So why did such a low-virulence flu break out?

A god told me the following very shortly after the outbreak of this flu in Mexico, on April 30, 2009:

Even though this new type of flu is only preliminary practice, it is not to be taken lightly. The low virulence is only for now. Viruses continue to live and multiply in living cells, and they continue to transform. It may be easier to think of the virus as one organism....

Chapter 4 The Future of Earth and Humanity

Because of that, it is possible that this virus could transform at any time from low virulence to high virulence. Living viruses not only have their own will, which causes them to keep multiplying, but they also have memory. They store the characteristics of anti viral drugs in their memory, and with further transformations, they can resist those drugs, and continue to multiply even further in the living cells of humans and animals. Humanity has so much confidence in themselves as the most righteous organism on the face of this Earth. From our perspective, though, this is downright laughable. We are praying that, by administering these warnings to overly-confident humanity, we may be able to increase the number of those whose souls are awakened, even if only by a few.

Right after I received this message from the god, in June of 2009, the virus was confirmed for the first time (in Denmark) to have mutated into a type resistant to the flu drug Tamiflu. Subsequently, the presence of this Tamiflu-resistant virus was confirmed in countries around the world, including Japan.

As the god has pointed out in the message, this new strain of the flu virus is a plague to warn humanity, which has become overly confident in itself. You may not believe that this is possible. Still, in actuality, the fact that the world is moving in the direction that the god has said is undeniable. This particular weak new strain of the flu virus is also a preliminary practice or simulation for the stronger strains of the virus that will eventually break out.

[30] As those who have taken part in one of my lectures before well know, I have been arguing in my lectures that it is crucial for us to take measures against a new strain of the flu virus, since deities revealed to me over a year before this outbreak that a new flu strain would break out. This outbreak means that this revelation has come true.

Fears of a highly virulent new flu strain

There are a variety of possible candidates in the running for what could become a new, highly virulent strain of the flu.

As the god indicated in the message above, the same new strain (H1N1) that had its origin as swine flu could potentially mutate to have much a higher level of virulence as it is transmitted from human to human. Currently, H1N1 has passed the peak of infection, and is in something of a state of remission.

Still, the possibility of second and even third waves of infection, with even higher virulence than before, cannot be denied.

There is also talk amongst experts that the outbreak of another new strain of the flu, H5N1, which originated as bird

Chapter 4 The Future of Earth and Humanity

flu, is only a matter of time. Right now, bird flu very rarely infects humans. But when it does, it is highly virulent, with a mortality rate of about 60 percent. Infection by this highly virulent strain originating from bird flu causes multiple organ failure. Many of those infected suffer from a high fever, coughing, convulsions, and other symptoms, and bleed out from their entire bodies, and then die.

Japan's Ministry of Health, Labour and Welfare predicts the deaths of an estimated 640,000 people if a new, highly virulent flu strain breaks out. In terms of Japan's population of roughly 128 million, this is calculated simply by assuming an infection rate of 25 percent, and a mortality rate of 2 percent. But considering that the current mortality rate for the bird flu is about 60 percent, it is hard to think that the mortality rate for a highly virulent strain could be this low of a number. Moreover, the US Department of Health and Human Services has estimated the rate of infection to be between 20 and 40 percent, and a mortality rate of 20 percent, ten times that of Japan's Ministry of Health, Labour and Welfare. If we apply these estimates to Japan's population, the dead would number over 6 million.

It is predicted that, if a pandemic involving a new, highly virulent strain of the flu, with more severe symptoms and higher mortality rates than the normal strain breaks out, the functions of society listed below will be paralyzed.

- Schools will be closed, all events canceled, and companies will restrain themselves from conducting business activities.
- Public transportation will be stopped.
- Hospital functions will be stopped (hospitals will overflow with patients to the point of bursting).
- There will be shortages of foodstuffs and other commodities necessary for daily life (due to stoppage of production lines and logistics).
- There will be stoppage of various "lifelines" (power, gas, water, and other utilities).

In addition to all of that, if a highly virulent strain like this causes a pandemic, there end up being bodies piled up in the streets. It is predicted that in Tokyo, if such a strain of the flu virus were to cause many deaths and exceed the capacity of crematoriums, public facilities like gymnasiums and sports centers would be used as temporary morgues. And then, if the capacity of those temporary morgues is also exceeded, consideration will be given to temporarily burying bodies in city parks and so on after sufficient sterilization.

So what can we do to protect ourselves from a highly viru-

Chapter 4 The Future of Earth and Humanity

lent new strain of the flu?

Two important points for protecting yourself are to not bring the infection into your household, and to avoid others from being infected. To do so, it is necessary to confine or quarantine yourself in your house. New strains of influenza are powerfully infectious. If this kind of flu virus outbreak occurs anywhere in the world, and if it does penetrate Japan, there is a possibility that it will spread throughout the country in the blink of an eye. For this reason, I would recommend that you begin to quarantine yourself in your own home in the event that the virus is confirmed to have entered Japan. As you will need to stay in your quarantine until the epidemic has passed, you will need to have at least about three months' worth of supplies at home including food and other daily necessities.[31]

---

[31] The Ministry of Health, Labour and Welfare recommends stockpiling two weeks' worth of provisions. According to many manuals written by experts on preventing new strains of flu (such as *Vaccine of Knowledge: Pandemic Influenza Prevention Manual,* advised by Harue Okada), two months' worth of provisions are recommended, but a god has told me that it will be necessary to stock up for three months in order to provide a margin.

Further fears of viruses

I've already discussed the threat of a new, highly virulent strain of the flu virus in some detail. The truth is, though, that

● **The direction of viruses**

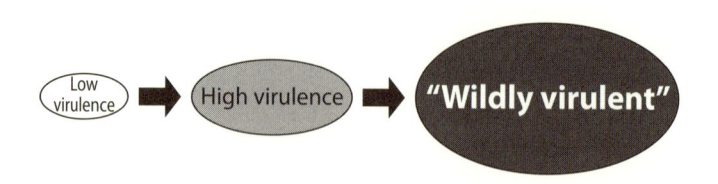

Low virulence → High virulence → "Wildly virulent"

new and stronger strains of the flu virus are just the very beginning. If a pandemic of new flu strains does indeed occur, many lives will be lost, and society will be thrown into a great confusion. But there will be a certain number of survivors. God and other deities have suggested that, if these survivors still do not change their hearts, however, they will unleash further warnings in the form of extremely lethal, unknown viruses on this Earth. (A god used the term "wildly virulent" regarding these viruses.) These wildly virulent viruses will not be treatable by any drug therapies, much less by current flu medicines like Tamiflu and Relenza, meaning that nearly 100 percent of those infected will die.

(2) Foot-and-mouth disease

As it occupied so much space in newspaper and television reports, I'm sure that my readers are aware of the foot-and-

Chapter 4 The Future of Earth and Humanity

mouth disease that spread among livestock in Miyazaki Prefecture, Japan from spring and into the summer of 2010.

According to God, foot-and-mouth disease is also a warning for humanity.

In regions where livestock (cattle, swine, and a small portion of goats) infected with the disease were found, large numbers of animals, including those that had not yet been infected, were destroyed. The scene of their destruction was like a snapshot of hell. The destruction was carried out using three methods: electric shock, lethal injections, and gas. Veterinarians destroyed the animals as they were herded by prefectural workers.

Of course, animals also have souls and feelings. This is why as this was going on, there were pigs who resisted, cows who met their destruction with sad, worried faces, and pigs squealing in sadness and pain. According to some sources, some of the workers even reported having seen some of the cows crying. Indeed, "hellish" is the best word to describe the gruesome scene. It was not only for the animals that this was difficult. The desolation of the farmers who had raised these livestock as their own children up to then is immeasurable. Besides that, despite the fact that it was their job, the sadness and fatigue of

● **The work of burying destroyed cows**

the veterinarians and other workers who had to destroy all of these animals in such cruel circumstances was indeed heavy.

The destroyed animals were all piled into a large hole that had been dug and then lined with a tarpaulin, and then buried. I have been told by a god that these gruesome scenes are meant to suggest the future of humanity, in which people will continue to die from diseases until funerals can no longer be held individually, and we are left with no choice but to either bury them together in large holes or pile them up to burn.

Chapter 4 The Future of Earth and Humanity

(3) Other infectious diseases

It's not just new types of influenza and foot-and-mouth disease, though. Ebola, dengue fever, AIDS, SARS, and on and on—these are all warnings given to arrogant humanity to make them understand their errors.

The Japanese sense of crisis is generally low, and most of them feel somehow that, in spite of all this, they will be fine—many feel that it is someone else's problem. But I would like to ask you to really stop and think hard for a minute about the fact that so many diseases are now sprouting up one after another. On top of that, new strains of flu and foot-and-mouth disease have already been happening close to home, in Japan. We are now getting closer to a world where we can wake up any day with a new disease having appeared on Earth, and you may catch it tomorrow.

(4) Protecting yourself from disease

In order to protect yourself from the various types of infectious diseases that will show up in the future, it is critical that you cleanse your body and build your immune system. Your immune system is basically the human body's natural power to heal itself. By building your immune system, you can prevent infiltration by viruses and bacteria, and you can also prevent the growth of cancerous cells. I'd like to introduce to you just three methods you can use to build your immune system.

Pay attention to the foods that you eat

Nearly all food products in Japan today are sullied by the use of food additives. Many of these additives are chemical substances. These can have all sorts of negative effects, including generating active oxygen in the body, causing allergies, and causing damage to cells. People who continue to take in these kinds of additives will have a weakened immune system before they have any clue what's going on.

So what can we do to make sure that we don't take in any more of these food additives?

The most crucial thing is to look at the ingredient labels of the foods you buy at the store (see above). The additives used in the food are all listed there. The large majority of people may be thinking, "Even looking at the label I don't know much about additives, so I'm not really sure." In that case, you can assume that anything that you don't recognize is an additive. You should do your best to try to choose foods with the least amount of additives in them.

In addition to additives, there is also danger in pesticide residues left on rice and vegetables, and meat from cattle and

Chapter 4 The Future of Earth and Humanity

● One example of ingredient labeling

Name	Sausage
Ingredients	pork, chicken, binding agents, reduced sugar syrup, salt, vegetable oils and fats, yeast extract, protein hydrolyzate, lactose, spices, soy sauce, modified starch, seasonings (amino acid, etc.), preservatives (potassium sorbate), phosphate (Na, K), pH adjuster, smoke flavoring solutions, spice extracts, antioxidants (vitamin C), color fixative (sodium nitrite), artificial colors (red 102, annatto, red 3)

swine raised using antibiotics. I would suggest that, from now on, you use organically produced rice and vegetables, and other natural foods.

Brown rice

In order to strengthen your immune system, you need to eat a balance of foods rich in different kinds of vitamins and nutrients. For that, brown rice is the best, as it has enough nutritional value to be called a "complete meal." Not only is brown rice high in nutritional value, but it also has the property of removing toxins from the body. It absorbs the toxins that have entered your body (additives, and pollutants from the environment), and moves them outside your body. Removing these toxins will strengthen your immune system.

Though brown rice is a wonderful food because of its rich nutrients and cleansing properties, it does have the drawback that it is hard to digest if you don't chew it very well. Try chewing between 50 and 100 times if you can. By chewing more, more saliva will be secreted, and produce an enzyme called peroxidase. This enzyme is to neutralize various carcinogens.

I would also recommend sprouted brown rice. When brown rice, which already is high in nutritional value, is sprouted, the value is increased even more. Further, because sprouted brown rice is easier to digest and tastes better than regular brown rice, it is relatively easier to eat.

I recommend replacing the white rice in one meal every day with brown rice, or even sprouted brown rice.

Drink at least two liters of water a day

To be healthy, drink at least 2 liters (about 64 ounces) of water every day.[32] About 60 percent of our body weight as adults is made up of water. By drinking plenty of water, your body will stimulate the creation of new cells to replace the old, and the old will be easier for your body to get rid of. The water can be normal tap water.[33] It could not also be high-temperature pasteurized mineral water.[34] With any kind of high-temperature pasteurized water, the inorganic substances, or oxygen and calcium and so on are reduced, so you can't expect any kind of effect. Avoid any kind of water that has been electro-

Chapter 4 The Future of Earth and Humanity

lyzed, ionized, or otherwise artificially processed.

Start by drinking a whole glass when you first wake up in the morning, and before you go to sleep at night. Outside of that, you can drink it little by little all day, as long as your total for the day is over 2 liters (about 64 ounces). Also, because your mouth is full of germs and bacteria when you first wake up, be sure to start drinking water after brushing your teeth or gargling.

These are a few ways in which you can cleanse your body and strengthen your immune system to protect yourself from infectious diseases. Be sure to understand, though, that these methods are at most self-defense measures. The diseases that are expected to appear in the future, however, are originally meant to be a warning against the wickedness of the hearts of humanity. For this reason, no matter how many measures you take to protect yourself, those who have wicked hearts from the divine perspective will catch these diseases with extreme ease.

What is really important is not just cleansing your body, but cleansing your heart and mind. (Ways to do this will be explained in the next section.) Only by cleansing *both* our hearts and our bodies can we truly protect ourselves from the diseases to come.

[32] The elderly and those with illness should drink water within a range that is safe for them.

[33] Tap water in Japan is chlorinated to kill bacteria. To remove the chlorine, I recommend either putting it through a filtration system, or letting it sit in a kettle for a short time.

[34] Much of the mineral water produced in Japan is high-temperature pasteurized (in rare cases you can find unpasteurized). Much of the mineral water produced outside Japan is bottled at the source, and so is unpasteurized.

4-6 How to survive: the importance of living with a righteous heart

As I have described, humankind is going to experience an extremely difficult period soon. Our Earth's environment will continue to deteriorate, natural disasters will keep happening one after another, there will be a worldwide depression and food shortages, along with the threat of a variety of infectious diseases. And this is all going to come to press on us at once. Many people will lose their lives. No matter how much we protest, we will be made aware of our own powerlessness.

I will not stop praying that even one more of you reading this book will be able to overcome these difficult times, and go on to bear the responsibility of the next civilization. That is why, in the final pages of this book, I will teach you how to live in order to survive these times. I hope that you will allow this

Chapter 4 The Future of Earth and Humanity

to serve as your guide for how to live your life from here on out.

What does it mean to live with a righteous heart?

As I keep repeating, the continual occurrences of various natural disasters and diseases are, in a sense, being brought about by God and other deities as a warning to humanity, whose hearts have grown wicked. On the other hand, those who will be left alive even after encountering all of these happenings, are those whose hearts God and other deities see as being pure.

So what does it mean to God and other deities for us as humans to have a pure heart?

In a phrase, it means "living with a righteous heart." Those who are pure and righteous of heart will always, without fail, be protected by God and other deities, no matter what circumstances they may meet. But what does it mean to live with a righteous heart? I'll explain it below.

(1) Do not live only to chase after money and material things

There are a great number of people in this world who seek only money and material possessions, and selfishly believe that it matters not what happens to others as long as they can make a profit for themselves. The number of people whose hearts stray in this way has increased, and, as a result of seeking profits, Earth's environment has been destroyed. You must now stop to listen to the cries of Earth, and repent your ways. From now on, rather than seeking money and possessions, live for the world, and live for others. By doing so, your heart and mind will be purified.

(2) Live in harmony with all things

This world (the Present Realm) is a place of practice where we cultivate our souls. The most important thing in cultivating your soul is to live in a way that is harmonious with others, no matter who they are, at home, at school, at work, and everywhere else. Many situations will require patience and forbearance in order to maintain harmony. You will also need to have kindness and consideration. By living in harmonious way, our souls improve markedly.

(3) Live to improve yourself

As humans, no matter what kind of person we may be, we all have a certain amount of bad habits and personality traits. When these sink in over long years, it can be rather hard to correct them. Still, we humans have been born in this world specifically to improve our souls. This is why deities hope that we will each look back on our lives up to now, and continue to

Chapter 4 The Future of Earth and Humanity

make an effort to correct our bad habits and traits (this is called "self-improvement").

In a sense, it could be said that the reason we are made to atone for our sins in the Astral Realm as we repeat the cycle of reincarnation and transmigration is to fix these bad habits and traits. These cause many people to sin in the course of their lives, and they are made to repent these sins in the Astral Realm. In order not to fall into the Astral Realm when we die, it is important to carry out this self-improvement right now, while we are alive.

(4) Believe in deities, and live with thanks for everything

As I explained in Chapter 3, we humans are brought to life by God and other deities as part of a grand scheme. If you trust in God and other deities who always watch over you, and live with a spirit of gratitude for everything, they will protect you from the various natural disasters and diseases that are going to occur.

There may be many among my readers who, looking back on their own lives, find that they have not had pure and righteous hearts. In our current world of materialist civilization, in a way, it is unavoidable. This is because, in our materialist culture, our unseen hearts have been neglected. What God and other deities are looking for, though, is for humanity to make the effort. It is more important to go forward by endeavoring to cleanse our hearts than to worry about what has happened up to now. Simply pray to deities that you want to be protected by them to survive, and want to be a part of building a new civilization (a spiritually-based civilization). If you do this, there is sure to be a brilliant future waiting for you as well.

In Closing

In this book, I have written that "the curtain will close on the civilization of this Earth."

How does this make my readers feel? There may be many of you who find it preposterous. God created this beautiful planet we call Earth long, long ago, and maintained an exquisite balance by adjusting natural forces, sustaining conditions in which humanity has been able to live comfortably until now.

We humans, however, have harvested every resource there is, greedily consuming Earth. A god has told me that the petroleum and all of the various ores in the ground were energy sources for the purpose of keeping Earth in its proper orbit around the sun. Humans, however, are trying to use all of these resources up. The very balance of Earth is about to come undone.

This internal balance of Earth being nearly destroyed, the magma inside it continues to activate, rising ever closer to the surface. In all locations, all over the world, volcanoes are working up to eruptions. From here on, even volcanoes thought to be dormant will erupt, much like Mount Sinabung on northern Sumatra that erupted for the first time in about 400 years.

This underground magma is being expelled little by little onto the surface of Earth, somehow just barely keeping the balance. This is the state that our Earth is currently in.

But the god has told me that, if the current civilization on this Earth continues on as it is, and we continue to destroy Earth's environment as we have up to now, at some point, being unable to withstand anymore, Earth itself will explode. If that happens, the entire universe will take on immense damage, and there will be no going back.

This is exactly the reason that the civilization currently on this Earth will be ended by God and other deities. This is incredibly similar to the conditions of the Mu civilization just before the continent of Mu sank. In that era as well, airplanes, missiles, and space rockets all existed. As civilization flourished, humanity came to believe too much in their own powers.

History repeats itself. Why has humanity brought all of this on itself?

This is because all of us are creatures of want and desire. Because we desire, we do progress, and we do develop. But what we need now is to give up on seeking money, possessions, and abundance beyond what is necessary, and begin to be thankful for what we have now. We must now stop and return to the origin of humanity, and change the way we have been living up to now.

Want not—
and then
you will find that what you have is plenty.

Want not—
and then
what you have now
will be vivid and exciting.

Want not—
and then
you will know that
you can live without more than you thought.

Want not—
and then
you will find yourself a little embarrassed
about what foolish things you wanted.

Want not—
and then

your mind, along with your body
will begin to relax.

Want not—
and then
time will start to pass more slowly.

(From "Want Not" in *Want Not* by Shozo Kajima, Shogakukan)

Since ancient times, the Japanese have been a people who have believed strongly in the worship of deities.

In recent years, however, because of crimes, money problems, and aggressive recruiting of certain religious groups, there are many who react negatively to the very mention of deities. In these times, it is inevitable, but it shows that Japan is in a very sad state. But the Almighty Creator of all things exists, completely unrelated to any specific religion. This is an undeniable fact. The Creator and other deities always love us, worry over us, and watch over us. The people of today, though, have simply chosen to forget deities and turn their eyes away.

Perhaps there will be some, both those who have always believed in deities, and those who haven't, who come to feel closer to God and other deities by reading this book. If the content of this book holds any interest for you, then please participate in one of the lectures we are now holding all over Japan. These lectures are not for the purpose of any kind of recruitment. Our intention is to pass on the things we have been taught by God to as many people as possible as we approach the final days of our civilization. To that end, we would like to ask you to introduce this book and our lectures to those around you.

In our lectures, we provide the latest information from deities in real time. I am convinced that, when you hear messages from deities at one of our lectures, your view on life will change. We also take questions from participants, and deities provides answers directly through the channeling of our spiritual counselor. Because deities answer directly, the solutions to riddles that we humans cannot possibly solve, the truth about mysterious and bizarre phenomena, the causes of serious illnesses and rare diseases, and the direction our Earth is headed in, will all be revealed.

These lectures have also been called "miracle lectures." That's because, by participating in our lectures, and scrutinizing and correcting the way they live, many people's lives have miraculously taken a turn for the better, or somehow their physical condition has improved. I ask all of my readers to try to get to one of our lectures to see and hear all of this for yourself.

As an author, there would be no greater joy than to bring as many people as possible to know of the existence of deities and the grand scheme for this universe, and to come through the end times of this civilization alive by taking another look at the way they have been living.

January 2011
Nichijo, on behalf of the Nichijo-kai

A note on the second edition

Since this book was first published in February of 2011, we have been blessed with many faithful readers. With its publication, the number of participants in our lectures has increased rapidly. Lately, the lectures have been so successful that the tickets sell out well before the lecture takes place, and long lines form outside the venues. I would like to take this opportunity to express my sincere thanks.

Even in 2011, we have seen large-scale disasters continue to occur with frequency, including the eruption of Shinmoedake, a volcano situated on the border between Kagoshima and Miyazaki Prefectures in Japan, the New Zealand earthquake, the Great East Japan Earthquake, and flooding in Thailand. Since before all of this happened, though, I have been transmitting in all kinds of ways the truths that deities have told me, including the prediction that "eruptions will happen starting from the southernmost tip of Kyushu," and that "the shaking will begin in Tohoku." Looking back on it now, it is clear that there were many things contained in my message that suggested the eruption of Shinmoedake and the Tohoku earthquake. The occurrence of these disasters in just the manner that deities have told me about them is terrifying even to me, the messenger.

From here on out, Earth's environment will deteriorate, and the occurrence of natural disasters and infectious diseases will increase. There are many, however, who will never stop praying for the protection of God and other deities, no matter what conditions they find themselves in.

Spring 2012

Author Profile
Nichijo
Born in Chiba Prefecture, Japan.
Nichijo received a revelation from God, and established the Nichijo-kai in 2004.
Currently, Nichijo works with spiritual counselor Kazuyo Omori, through whose channeling he can converse with deities directly. His work is to guide the members of the Nichijo-kai, and conduct lectures all over Japan.
Guidance to members involves nuanced, individualized advice on how to live, and counseling for troubles and anxiety. In his lectures, Nichijo shares the teachings he has received from God to ordinary folks, on issues like the death and rebirth of humanity, the correct way for us to live as humans, the future of Earth and humankind, and the laws of the universe. People are rushing to these lectures, where Nichijo provides the latest updates in real time on predictions.

*The origin of Nichijo's name
Nichijo is said to be the reincarnation of the Venerable Nichijo (1269-1342), a priest who lived in the Kamakura period around 700 years ago, and who was celebrated on par with the Venerable Nichiren and the Venerable Nichiro. In the Kamakura period, Nichijo propagated Nichiren Buddhism in Japan, and laid the foundations of that school by obtaining the official recognition of the Emperor, which was not an easy task. In 1293, he resolved to preach the gospel in Kyoto, in accordance with Nichiren's dying wishes. He had the support of the masses in Kyoto, but, facing oppression by Hieizan Enryakuji Temple, he was exiled from the capital three times. Each time he was pardoned, and in 1321 he returned to Kyoto to found the temple, Myokenji Temple.

For information on participating in lectures, please contact "Arigato Chikyu-go."
http://www.ari-gato.org/ (in Japanese)

The Truth Never Hitherto Disclosed

2012年9月18日　初版第1刷発行

著　者　Nichijo
発行者　韮澤　潤一郎
発行所　株式会社 たま出版
　　　　〒160-0004 東京都新宿区四谷4-28-20
　　　　　　☎ 03-5369-3051（代表）
　　　　　　http://tamabook.com
　　　　　　振替　00130-5-94804

組　版　一企画
印刷所　株式会社エーヴィスシステムズ

©Nichijo　2012　Printed in Japan
ISBN978-4-8127-0349-6　C0011